VIETNAM JOURNAL

BOOK SEVEN - VALLEY OF DEATH

CALIBER
COMICS

BOOK SEVEN - VALLEY OF DEATH

Written and Illustrated
By
DON LOMAX

Inks by
ROSE LOMAX

Lettered
By
AGNES PINAHA

**This volume collects the Vietnam Journal Valley of Death
series issues 1-4, and the Vietnam Journal Hamburger Hill serial**

VIETNAM JOURNAL

MY BY-LINE READS: SCOTT
NEITHAMMER, BUT THE TROOPS
CALL ME "JOURNAL."

"UP THE A SHAU"

Team "Red" comes in righteous, its gunships bristling for a fight, mean and green, nap of the earth!

The "Hawks", team "white", on their flanks, are there to stir up as much trouble as possible and draw enemy fire!

And following up the rear, team "Blue", locked and cocked and ready to rock. The Blanket Brigade's 11 Bravo, ready to kick ass and to hell with their names!

The A Shau Valley. A wide, lush valley located in I Corps near the Laotian Border. This remote haven for the North Vietnamese Army was extensively used as a staging area throughout the Vietnam War to infiltrate men and materiel into the South from the enemy's sanctuaries in Laos.

A beautiful, deadly, forbidding place that the NVA know as well as they know the backs of their own individual hands. Soon the peaceful quiet of the valley will erupt and the jungle will blossom with dozens of white smoke trails knifing out like cotton candy dispensers of death toward the American gunships from RPGs and rockets positioned in every viable hiding place imaginable.

Hell has come to the A Shau.

Vietnam Journal
Valley of Death
DEATH

BLOOD STRIPE

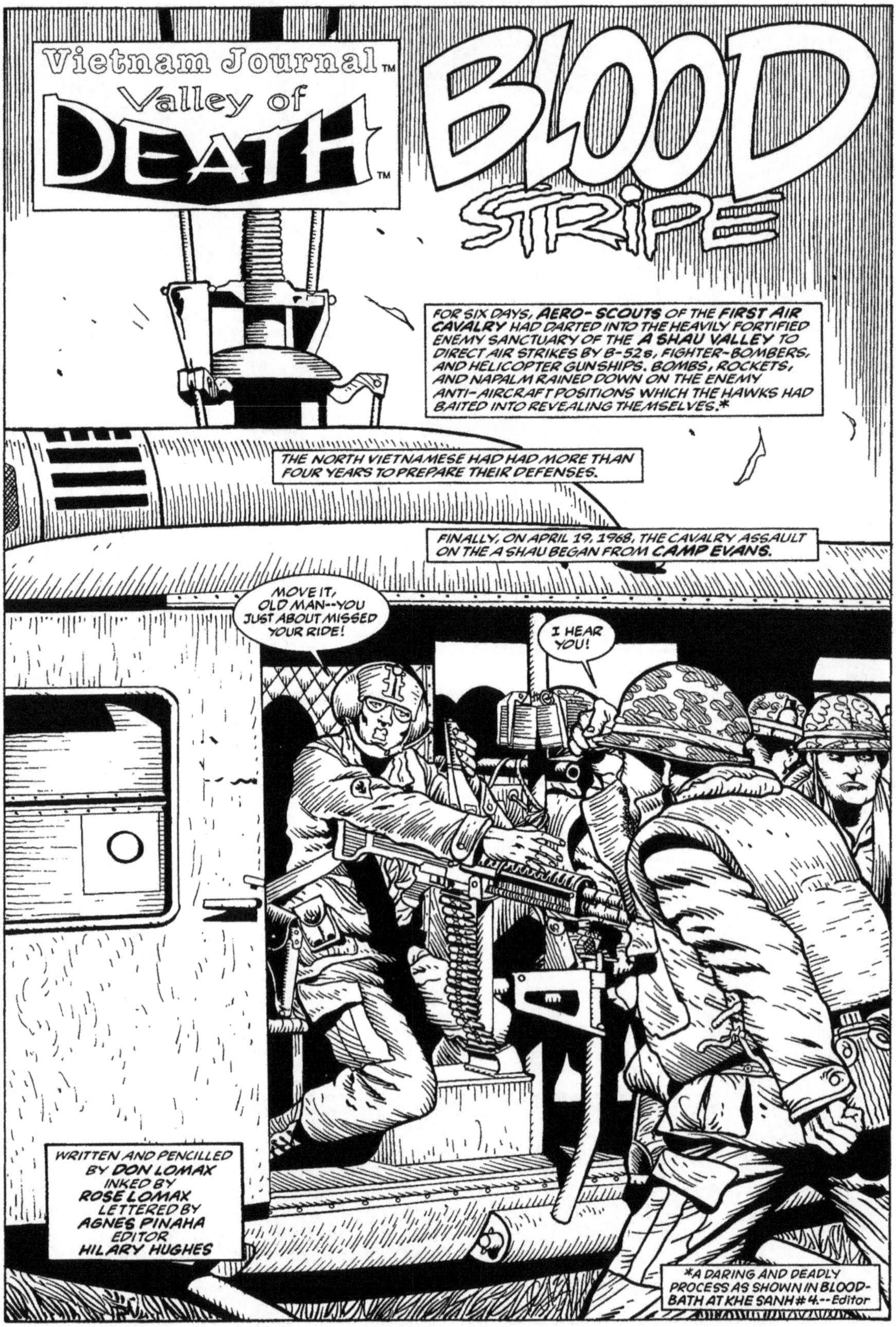
Vietnam Journal™
Valley of DEATH™
BLOOD STRIPE
FOR SIX DAYS, AERO-SCOUTS OF THE FIRST AIR CAVALRY HAD DARTED INTO THE HEAVILY FORTIFIED ENEMY SANCTUARY OF THE A SHAU VALLEY TO DIRECT AIR STRIKES BY B-52s, FIGHTER-BOMBERS, AND HELICOPTER GUNSHIPS. BOMBS, ROCKETS, AND NAPALM RAINED DOWN ON THE ENEMY ANTI-AIRCRAFT POSITIONS WHICH THE HAWKS HAD BAITED INTO REVEALING THEMSELVES.*
THE NORTH VIETNAMESE HAD HAD MORE THAN FOUR YEARS TO PREPARE THEIR DEFENSES.
FINALLY, ON APRIL 19, 1968, THE CAVALRY ASSAULT ON THE A SHAU BEGAN FROM CAMP EVANS.
MOVE IT, OLD MAN--YOU JUST ABOUT MISSED YOUR RIDE!
I HEAR YOU!
WRITTEN AND PENCILLED BY DON LOMAX INKED BY ROSE LOMAX LETTERED BY AGNES PINAHA EDITOR HILARY HUGHES
*A DARING AND DEADLY PROCESS AS SHOWN IN BLOODBATH AT KHE SANH #4.--Editor

THIS WAS NOT THE STREETS OF HUÉ NOR A LIGHTNING ASSAULT TO OPEN ROUTE 9 TO KHE SANH. THIS WAS DOWNTOWN "CHARLIEVILLE." WE WERE TAKING THE WAR TO THE ENEMY IN THE TRUEST SENSE OF THE PHRASE.

WAIT A MINUTE. SOMEBODY ELSE COMING.

IVERSEN, LAURENCE E., PUBLIC INFORMATION OFFICE.

THANKS.

YOU MAY REGRET MAKING THIS FLIGHT IN A SHORT SHORT, SARGE.

TICKETS, PLEASE.

UNH?

SCOTT NEITHAMMER, FREELANCE.

I COULD HARDLY HEAR HIM ABOVE THE DRONE OF HUNDREDS OF REVVING TURBINE ENGINES.

AS THE ROTORS SCREWED US INTO THE AIR, SMALL TALK DOMINATED. IT WAS BETTER THAN THINKING ABOUT WHAT WAS TO COME.

WE ZIGZAGGED AMONG THE CLOUD-COVERED PEAKS LIKE A SWARM OF GIANT DRAGONFLIES. CHINOOKS, LOADED WITH SUPPORT, BROUGHT UP THE REAR.

AHEAD, BEYOND OUR VISION, THE HAWKS WERE ON POINT, AS ALWAYS.

SO-- HOW LONG HAVE YOU BEEN WITH THE CAV, P.I.O.?

LESS THAN A MONTH. I WAS WITH THE 11TH INFANTRY, AMERICAL DIVISION.

WHERE'D YOU COME FROM?

KHE SANH.

BUMMER.

FREELANCE, HUH? THAT'S WHAT I WANT TO DO WHEN I GROW UP.

I ENVY YOU.

HOW'S THAT?

POLITICS, FRIEND. WHEN YOU'RE AN ARMY COMBAT PHOTOGRAPHER, YOU GO WHERE YOU'RE TOLD TO GO, TAKE THE PICTURES YOU'RE TOLD TO TAKE, AND SEE ONLY WHAT YOU'RE TOLD YOU SAW.

POLITICS.

I'D HAD A CHANCE TO TALK TO A COUPLE OF HAWKS OVER MY OATMEAL THAT MORNING. *W.O.s TROOP AND BOYD* HAD BEEN IN THE A SHAU SINCE THE 14TH, AND HAD SOME HAIR-RAISING STORIES TO TELL.

A 45-KILOMETER SLASH IN THE RUGGED MOUNTAINS NEXT TO THE LAOTIAN BORDER IN *THUA THIEN PROVINCE,* THE A SHAU IS A LOGISTICS NIGHTMARE.

THE VALLEY FLOOR IS A SEEMINGLY IMPENETRABLE TANGLE OF SCRUB THICKETS AND ELEPHANT GRASS, THREE KILOMETERS ACROSS AT ITS WIDEST POINT. THE MOUNTAINS ABOVE ARE LOST IN THICK, LOW-HANGING CLOUDS MOST OF THE TIME.

ON THE SLOPES, AA TO THE RIGHT OF US, AA TO THE LEFT OF US. IT WAS A VICIOUS, CLOSE-IN SHOOTING GALLERY.

AND WE WERE RIDING STRAIGHT INTO IT. INTO THE *VALLEY OF DEATH.*

THEIRS NOT TO REASON WHY...

THEIRS BUT TO DO AND...

IT WAS THE WRONG TIME TO BE QUOTING TENNYSON.

ONLY THE HIGHEST PEAKS WERE VISIBLE AS WE DESCENDED INTO THE CLINGING CLOUDS. THE TARGET WAS THE ABANDONED SPECIAL FORCES AIRSTRIP AT *CAMP A LOUI.* NO ONE SPOKE. MOUTHS WERE DRY. PALMS WERE SWEATY.

THE ONLY SOUNDS OVER THE ROAR OF THE ROTORS WERE THE METALLIC CLANK OF M-16 BOLTS CHAMBERING ROUNDS AND THE M-60s BEING CHARGED.

THEN THE SHIT HIT. RED TEAMS RADIOED A BUZZSAW OF FLAK. SEVERAL OF THEIR SHIPS WERE ALREADY CRASHING IN FLAMES.

IT WAS TOO MUCH TO LAND. SLICKS GLUTTED WITH TROOPS. PLANS HAD TO CHANGE -- FAST. COMMAND DECIDED TO DIVERT TO AN ALTERNATE LZ.

SKYBURSTS WERE FLOWERING EVERYWHERE.

I COULD FEEL THE SHOCK WAVES ROCK THE HUEY AND HEAR THE FLAK PEPPER THE THIN SKIN LIKE RAIN ON A TIN ROOF.

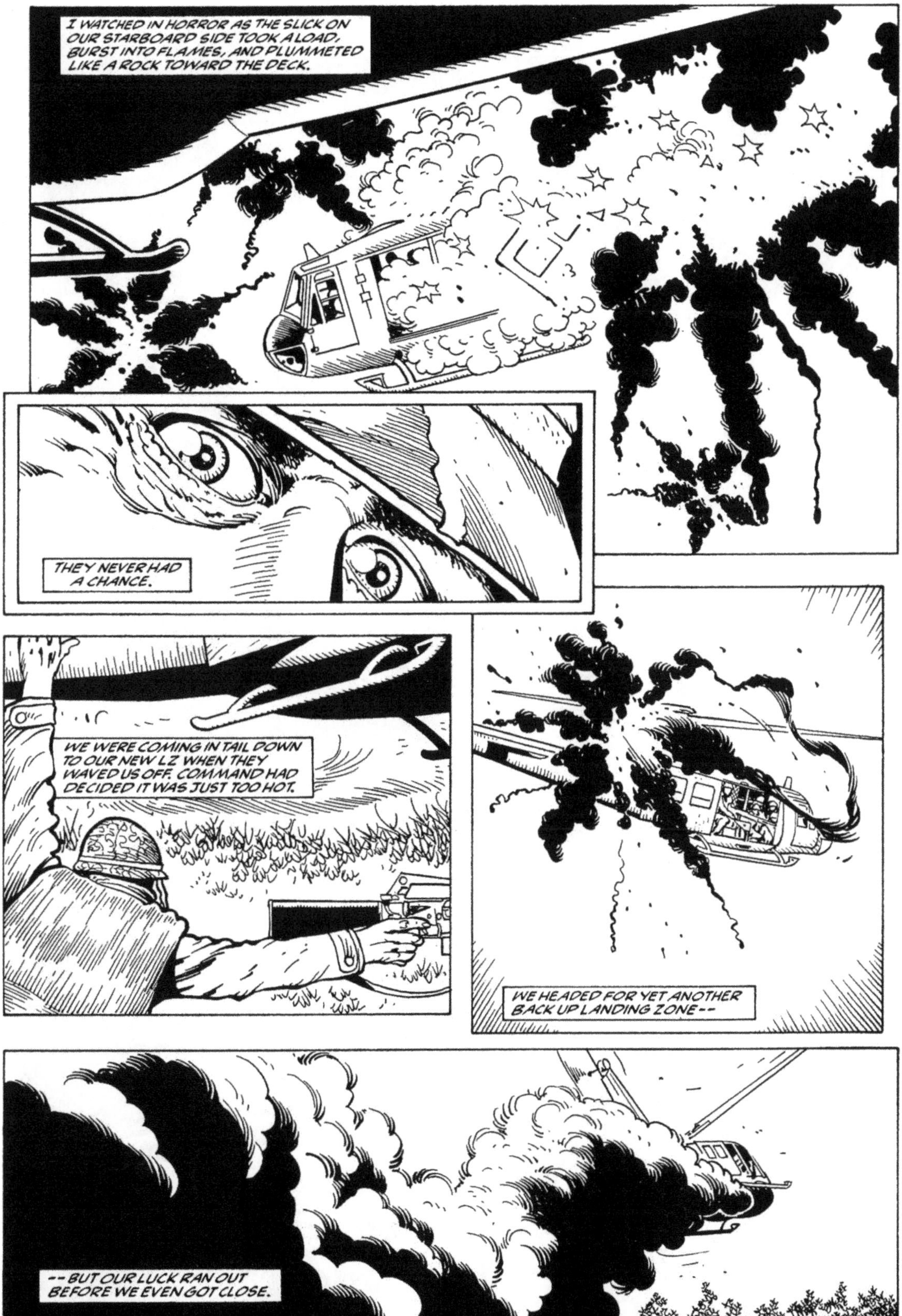
I WATCHED IN HORROR AS THE SLICK ON OUR STARBOARD SIDE TOOK A LOAD, BURST INTO FLAMES, AND PLUMMETED LIKE A ROCK TOWARD THE DECK.
THEY NEVER HAD A CHANCE.
WE WERE COMING IN TAIL DOWN TO OUR NEW LZ WHEN THEY WAVED US OFF. COMMAND HAD DECIDED IT WAS JUST TOO HOT.
WE HEADED FOR YET ANOTHER BACK UP LANDING ZONE--
--BUT OUR LUCK RAN OUT BEFORE WE EVEN GOT CLOSE.

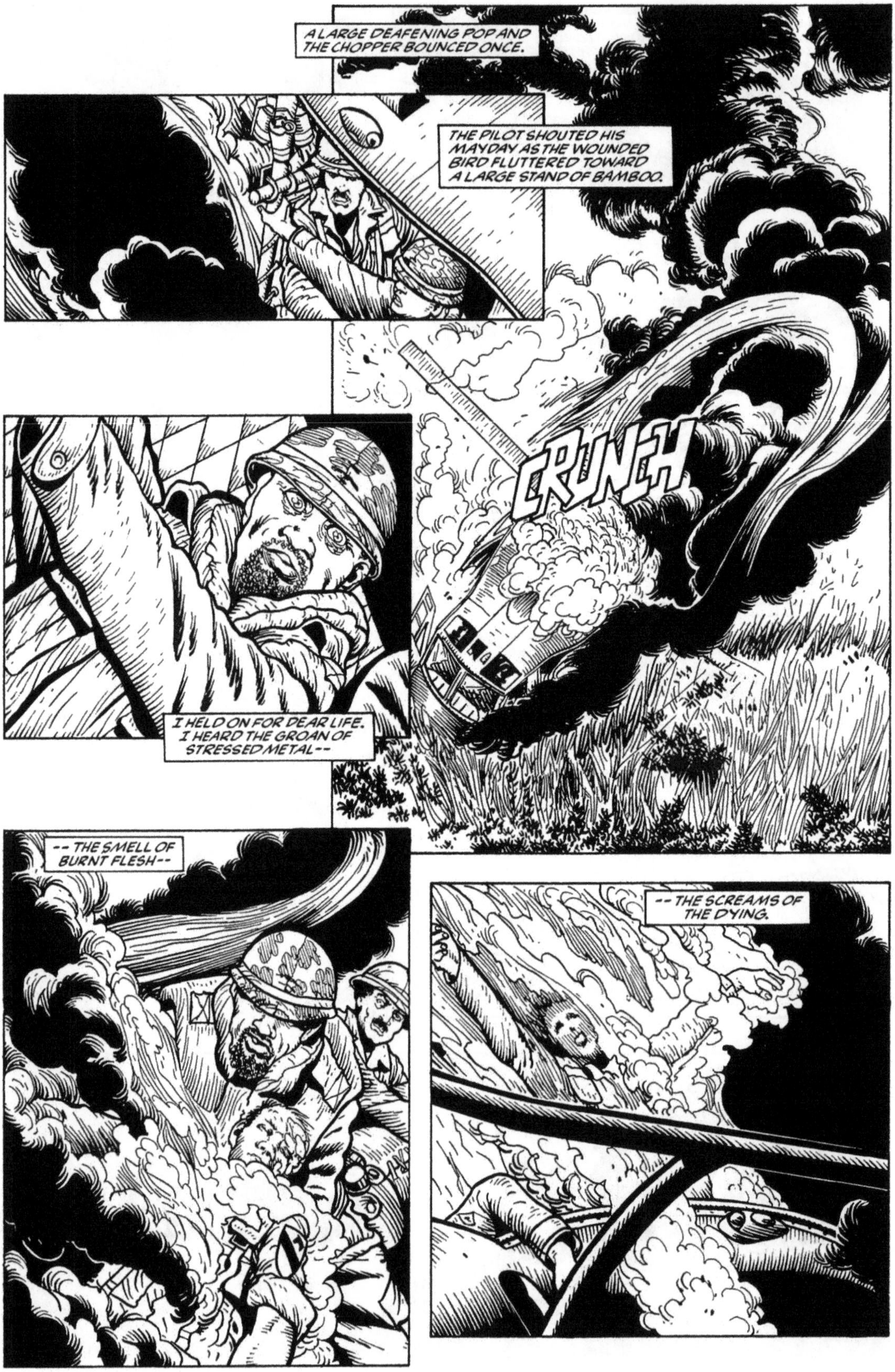
A LARGE DEAFENING POP AND THE CHOPPER BOUNCED ONCE.
THE PILOT SHOUTED HIS MAYDAY AS THE WOUNDED BIRD FLUTTERED TOWARD A LARGE STAND OF BAMBOO.
I HELD ON FOR DEAR LIFE. I HEARD THE GROAN OF STRESSED METAL--
CRUNCH
-- THE SMELL OF BURNT FLESH--
-- THE SCREAMS OF THE DYING.

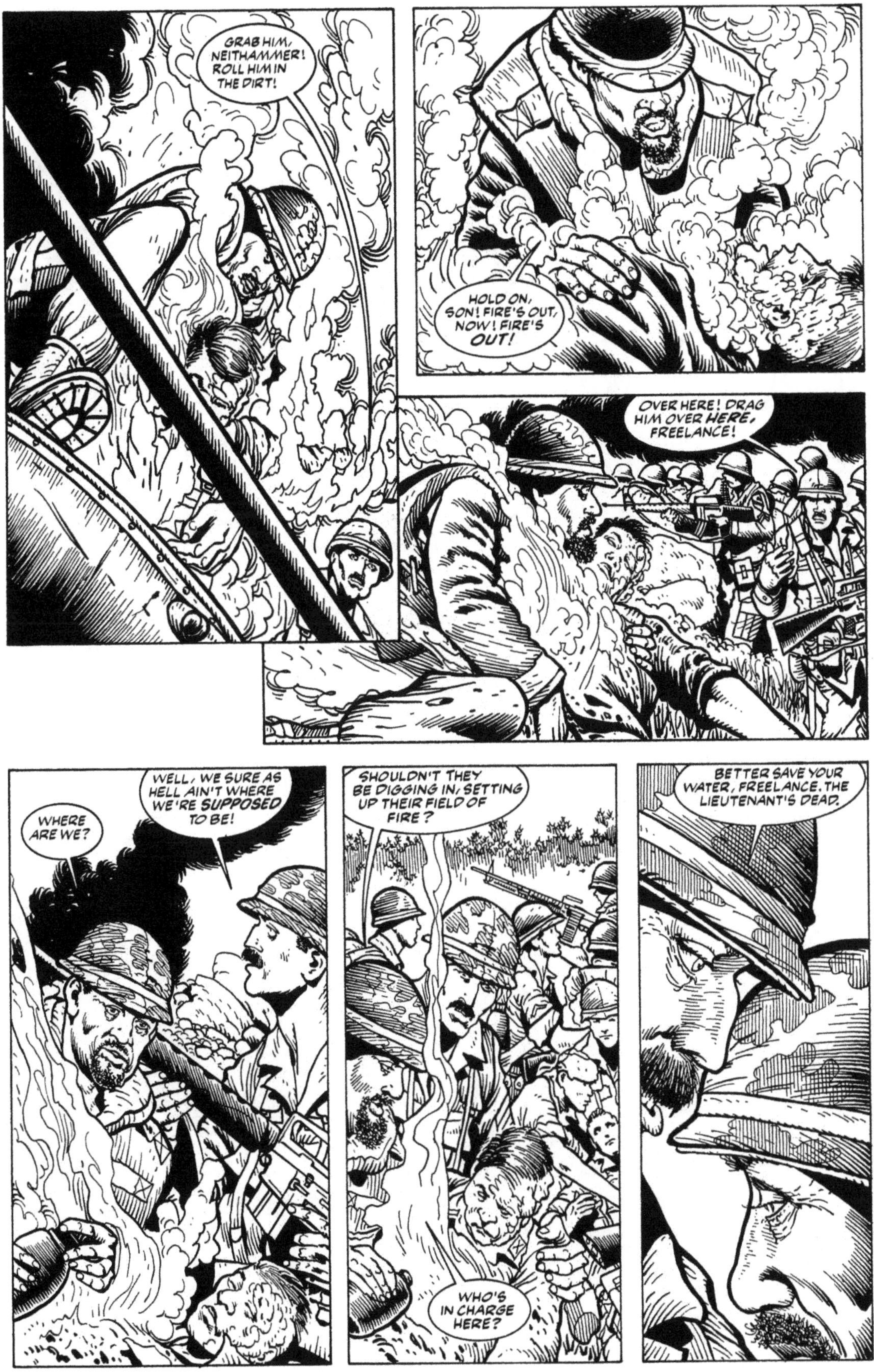
GRAB HIM, NEITHAMMER! ROLL HIM IN THE DIRT!
HOLD ON, SON! FIRE'S OUT, NOW! FIRE'S OUT!
OVER HERE! DRAG HIM OVER HERE, FREELANCE!
WHERE ARE WE?
WELL, WE SURE AS HELL AIN'T WHERE WE'RE SUPPOSED TO BE!
SHOULDN'T THEY BE DIGGING IN, SETTING UP THEIR FIELD OF FIRE?
WHO'S IN CHARGE HERE?
BETTER SAVE YOUR WATER, FREELANCE. THE LIEUTENANT'S DEAD.

JOURNAL.

HUH?

JOURNAL. THEY CALL ME JOURNAL.

YEAH. WELL, IT LOOKS LIKE I'M THE RANKING NCO HERE UNTIL HELP COMES.

IF HELP COMES.

SARGE, WE'RE IN A WORLD OF SHIT-- WE'RE AT THE WRONG END OF THE VALLEY.

WE'VE GOT SURVIVORS FROM THE OTHER SLICKS AND GUNSHIPS THAT WERE SHOT DOWN. WE'LL CONGREGATE, SET UP A PERIMETER, AND WAIT FOR INSTUCTIONS.

MAYBE ONE OF THE OTHER TEAMS HAS A WORKING RADIO TELEPHONE.

MAYBE THERE'LL BE SOMEBODY WHO OUTRANKS ME.

I HOPE TO HELL SO.

BUT AT THE OTHER END OF THE VALLEY, THE 1/7 WAS IN NO POSITION TO RESCUE ANYBODY.

THEIR MISSION WAS TO ESTABLISH A FIREBASE WHICH WOULD BE USED TO COORDINATE A PUSH TO SECURE THE A SHAU VALLEY ALL THE WAY TO *A LOUI.*

PINNED UNDER FIRE FROM THE MOUNTAINS ON BOTH SIDES AND BURDENED WITH HEAVY CASUALTIES, ALL THEY COULD MANAGE WAS TO DIG IN AND WAIT FOR THE FIRESTORM TO SUBSIDE.

BUT THE RAIN OF ARTILLERY AND MORTAR SHELLS SHOWED NO SIGN OF LETTING UP ANY TIME SOON.

THE *5TH BATTALION* JOINED THE BATTLE.

THEY ALSO LANDED UNDER ENEMY FIRE--

--AND DUG IN.

DURING THE NEXT TWO HOURS, WE STRENGTHENED OUR POSITION.

OUR NUMBER HAD GROWN BY SEVEN-- STRAGGLERS FROM ANOTHER DOWNED CHOPPER.

FOUR OF THE SEVEN WERE WOUNDED, TWO VERY SERIOUSLY.

BUT OF THE THREE ABLE-BODIED, A TREASURE! AN UNINJURED RADIO/TELEPHONE OPERATOR!

THE BAD NEWS FOR SSGT. IVERSEN-- HE REMAINED THE RANKING NCO.

ALL RIGHT, CORPORAL, GET A COUPLE OF PEOPLE OUT THERE AND CUT BACK SOME OF THAT BAMBOO TO IMPROVE OUR FIELD OF FIRE!

RT! GET ME BATTALION ON THE HORN.

THE WORD FROM BATTALION WAS LESS THAN SUPPORTIVE: HANG TIGHT. DIG IN. WE'LL GET TO YOU.

RIGHT.

BY AFTERNOON, THE **1ST BATTALION** HAD CUT A LANDING ZONE LARGE ENOUGH TO HANDLE CHINOOKS -- HAULING 105mm BATTERY PIECES AND LARGE PALLETS OF AMMO.

THE NVA LET LOOSE A HAIL OF MORTARS TO STOP THE DELIVERIES.

POOT

THA-BOOM

BUT, LIKE THE POST OFFICE, THE CHINOOKS GOT THEIR PACKAGES THROUGH.

BOOM

WITHIN MOMENTS, THE GROUND CREWS BEGAN A SPECIAL "RETURN TO SENDER" CAMPAIGN OF THEIR OWN.

BROON

EVENING FELL AND THE CLAMMY MISTS CLOSED IN. THE POSSIBILITY OF SLEEP SEEMED REMOTE. FIRES WERE OUT OF THE QUESTION.

IT WASN'T ONLY THE DAMP THAT CHILLED ME TO THE BONE. THE LOW, CHOKING MOANS OF THE WOUNDED AND THE DWINDLING OF FOOD, POTABLE WATER, AND AMMUNITION WERE JUST AS BLEAK.

BATTALION SAYS TO KEEP A LOW PROFILE AND REPORT TROOP MOVEMENTS THROUGH THIS SECTOR. THEY SAY THEY'LL UNDATE US IN THE A.M.

OUR NUMBER WAS DOWN TO TWELVE. TWO OF THE MOST SERIOUSLY INJURED HAD DIED THAT AFTERNOON.

IN BETWEEN THE MORTARS, I'VE HEARD 'HOOKS' GOIN' UP THE VALLEY ALL GODDAMN DAY. WHY CAN'T THEY TOUCH-AND-GO HERE AND HAUL THESE WOUNDED OUT?

LOOK, SPECIALIST, I JUST TAKE PICTURES. I'VE DONE EVERYTHING I CAN HERE SHORT OF KISSING LYNDON JOHNSON'S ASS IN THE ROSE BOWL PARADE.

THEY SAY THEY'LL BEGIN A PUSH TOWARD US FIRST THING IN THE MORNING. THAT'S ALL I KNOW.

THE DARKNESS WAS CONTINUALLY PUNCTUATED BY ARTILLERY FLASHES AND THE CONSTANT FLICKERING OF FLARES FARTHER UP THE VALLEY.

DON'T USE THOSE FLARES UNLESS YOU HAVE TO. THEY'RE ALL WE HAVE.

FROM THE CROSSTALK ON THE RADIO, THERE'S ONE HELL OF AN ARTILLERY DUEL GOING ON AT THE NORTH END OF THE VALLEY.

YEAH. I HAVEN'T SEEN ANYTHING BUT I'VE GOT A FEELING THAT THEIR TROOPS HAVE BEEN MOVING PAST US, HEADING UP THAT WAY ALL EVENING.

GOTTA BE.

WE'RE NOT THE ONLY ONES LOST OUT HERE. BATTALION WILL COLLECT US IN THE MORNING.

PRETTY HAIRY AT KHE SANH?

IT HAD ITS MOMENTS.

HOW'D YOU MANAGE TO LAND A JOB AS COMBAT PHOTOGRAPHER? WERE YOU A NEWSPAPERMAN BACK IN THE WORLD?

HUH? OH, NO -- FAR FROM IT.

MY M.O.S. IS 37-BRAVO. WHEEL AND TRACK VEHICLE MECHANIC.

MECHANIC?

SURE. THIS IS THE ARMY, MAN.

THE LONG NIGHT DRAGGED ON. EXCEPT FOR THE SERIOUSLY INJURED, WE WERE 50% ON WATCH, 50% OFF.

THE MIST HAD THICKENED TO A LOW, STIFLING FOG. I HAD NO WAY OF KNOWING WHAT TIME IT WAS. I COULDN'T RISK LIGHTING UP MY WATCH.

SSGT. IVERSEN DOZED.

MMMMUMM... NNN--MUM...

NO! NO!

IVERSEN! WAKE UP, MAN! YOU'RE DREAMING!

HUH? UMMM.

GHOSTS?

YEAH -- YEAH, I GUESS SO.

SOME SHIT WENT DOWN LAST MONTH WHEN I WAS WITH THE AMERICAL DIVISION. I'VE BEEN A COMBAT PHOTOGRAPHER FOR EIGHT MONTHS, BUT I AIN'T NEVER SEEN NOTHING LIKE IT.

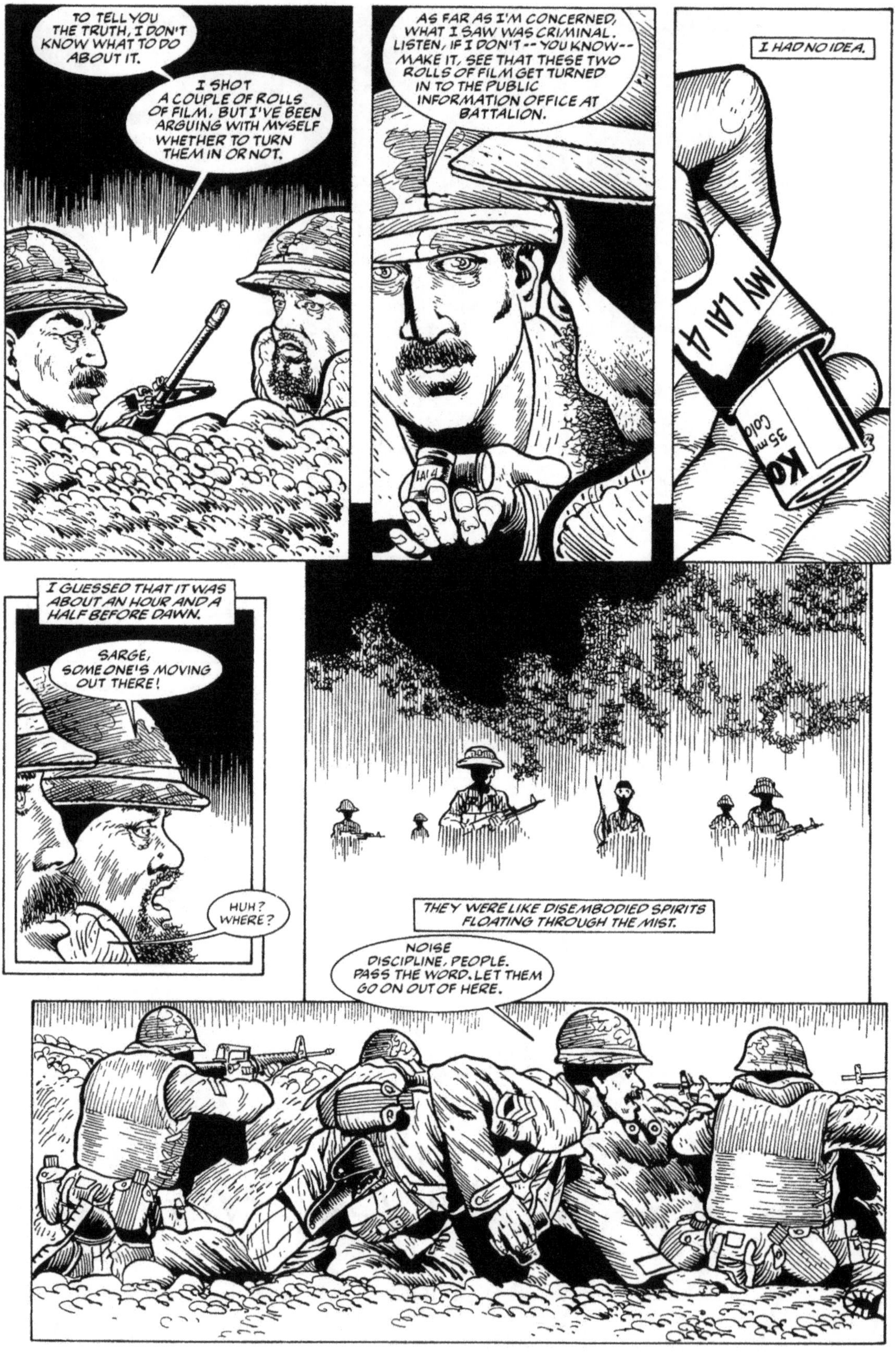
TO TELL YOU THE TRUTH, I DON'T KNOW WHAT TO DO ABOUT IT.
I SHOT A COUPLE OF ROLLS OF FILM, BUT I'VE BEEN ARGUING WITH MYSELF WHETHER TO TURN THEM IN OR NOT.
AS FAR AS I'M CONCERNED, WHAT I SAW WAS CRIMINAL. LISTEN, IF I DON'T -- YOU KNOW -- MAKE IT, SEE THAT THESE TWO ROLLS OF FILM GET TURNED IN TO THE PUBLIC INFORMATION OFFICE AT BATTALION.
I HAD NO IDEA.
MY LAI 4
I GUESSED THAT IT WAS ABOUT AN HOUR AND A HALF BEFORE DAWN.
SARGE, SOME ONE'S MOVING OUT THERE!
HUH? WHERE?
THEY WERE LIKE DISEMBODIED SPIRITS FLOATING THROUGH THE MIST.
NOISE DISCIPLINE, PEOPLE. PASS THE WORD. LET THEM GO ON OUT OF HERE.

I'M NOT SURE EXACTLY WHAT HAPPENED NEXT. A NOISE. METAL AGAINST METAL.

CLANK

THEY FLOATED TOWARD US. THE JIG WAS UP?

SHIT.

YEAH.

SOMEONE OPENED UP, A COUPLE OF HOLES DOWN FROM US--

BA DAP

-- INSTANT INSANITY!

TA DOW DOW DOW

PA DOW DOW

THE HANDFUL OF SKY SOLDIERS, HOPING TO APPEAR TO BE A LARGER FORCE THAN THEY REALLY WERE, THREW AN IMPRESSIVE WALL OF LEAD AT THE ADVANCING ENEMY.

BA BAP

BA BAP

BA BA BA BAP

BAD

BA DAP

BA BA BAP

BA BA BAP

EVEN AMONG THE SERIOUSLY WOUNDED, THOSE WHO COULD DRAGGED THEMSELVES INTO POSITION TO RETURN FIRE.

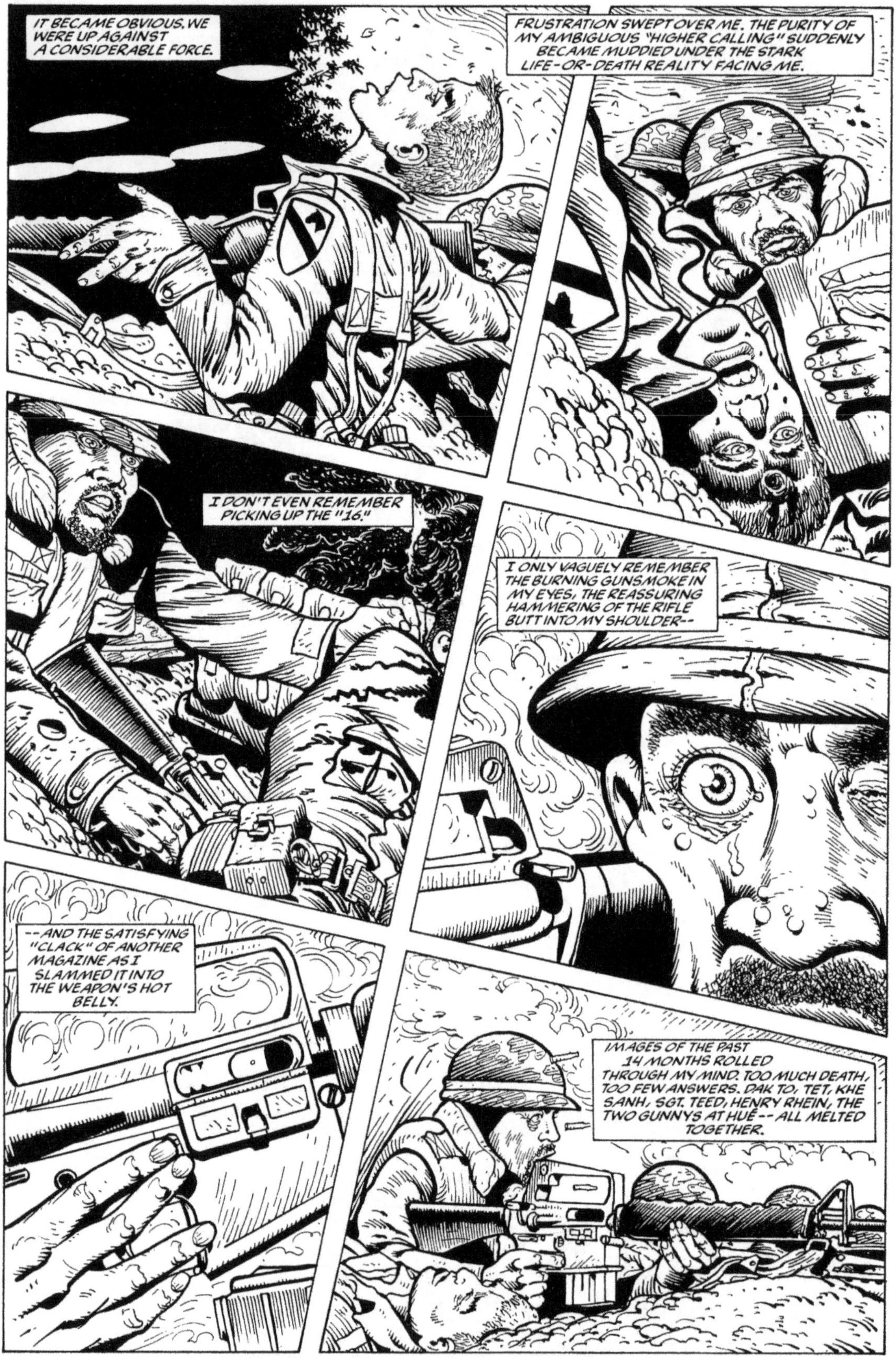
IT BECAME OBVIOUS. WE WERE UP AGAINST A CONSIDERABLE FORCE.
FRUSTRATION SWEPT OVER ME. THE PURITY OF MY AMBIGUOUS "HIGHER CALLING" SUDDENLY BECAME MUDDIED UNDER THE STARK LIFE-OR-DEATH REALITY FACING ME.
I DON'T EVEN REMEMBER PICKING UP THE "16."
I ONLY VAGUELY REMEMBER THE BURNING GUNSMOKE IN MY EYES, THE REASSURING HAMMERING OF THE RIFLE BUTT INTO MY SHOULDER--
--AND THE SATISFYING "CLACK" OF ANOTHER MAGAZINE AS I SLAMMED IT INTO THE WEAPON'S HOT BELLY.
IMAGES OF THE PAST 14 MONTHS ROLLED THROUGH MY MIND. TOO MUCH DEATH, TOO FEW ANSWERS. DAK TO, TET, KHE SANH, SGT. TEED, HENRY RHEIN, THE TWO GUNNYS AT HUÉ-- ALL MELTED TOGETHER.

MAYBE I WAS SICK OF THE SIDELINES AND WANTED TO GET INTO THE GAME. I'D RATHER BELIEVE I WAS COMING TO THE AID OF MY COUNTRY/MEN.

I DIDN'T HAVE TIME TO ANALYZE MY MOTIVES. PERHAPS IT WAS MORE BASIC THAN THAT. PERHAPS IT WAS SURVIVAL.

SSGT. IVERSEN'S FRANTIC, REPEATED PLEAS FOR HELP OVER THE RT FINALLY BROUGHT GUNSHIPS.

WHILE TWO HUEY "HOGS" LIT UP THE JUNGLE--

-- A CHINOOK SET DOWN 50 METERS FROM US.

IVERSEN! IVERSEN, TIME TO GET YOUR PEOPLE TOGETH--

--IVERSEN?!

YOU OKAY, MAN?

WE GOTTA GO. THE GUNSHIPS WON'T BE ABLE TO HOLD 'EM BACK FOREVER.

C'MON, OLDTIMER! CHARLIE'S GONNA BE ON US LIKE STINK ON SHIT ASAP.

WAIT A MINUTE.

WHAT'RE THOSE, MAN?

I DON'T KNOW. ALL I KNOW IS THAT I PROMISED HIM I'D DELIVER THEM TO HIS HOME OFFICE AT BRIGADE HEADQUARTERS.

WILCOX

US ARMY

IT WAS THE MORNING OF APRIL 20TH. WE HAD BEEN IN THE A SHAU LESS THAN 24 HOURS. THE LOSS OF MEN AND EQUIPMENT WAS ALREADY SUBSTANTIAL.

I DID NOT SHED ANY TEARS FOR IVERSEN. WHAT I HAD BEEN THROUGH THE PAST FEW MONTHS HAD LEFT ME NUMB -- AND RESIGNED TO THE LOSS OF PEOPLE CLOSE TO ME.

CONSCIOUSLY OR NOT, I HAD BEGUN TO AVOID INVESTING EMOTIONALLY IN ANY MORE RELATIONSHIPS.

I FULFILLED MY PROMISE. I LEFT THE FILM WITH A BATTALION CLERK AT CAMP EVANS, TO BE FORWARDED TO SSGT. IVERSEN'S OFFICE. I HEARD NOTHING ABOUT IT AFTER THAT.

ORDERLY ROOM

HAD I SUSPECTED THE IMPORTANCE OF WHAT WAS ON IT, I MIGHT HAVE FOLLOWED UP.

AS IT WAS, I NEVER THOUGHT ABOUT IVERSEN'S FILM AGAIN UNTIL THE FOLLOWING SPRING, WHEN DETAILS OF THE MY LAI MASSACRE CAME TO LIGHT.

I RETURNED TO THE A SHAU.

THAT SAME MORNING, APRIL 20, THE FIRST OF THE SEVENTH AND THE 5/7TH BEGAN THEIR PUSH ACROSS THE VALLEY FLOOR. THE WAR WENT ON -- AND ON.

NEXT: SANCTUARY!

Missing American

Bird Dog down, Captain Hugh Byrd and First Lieutenant Kevin O'Brien **MIA**

The following profiles two of those Missing Americans:

On January 9, 1969, Captain Hugh Byrd, pilot, and 1Lt. Kevin O'Brien, observer. were on a visual reconnaissance mission over the Khe Sanh area of South Vietnam in an O1g Bird Dog aircraft. Byrd's aircraft flew from the 200th Aviation Company, 212th Aviation Battalion, 94th Artillery, to identify artillery targets. The plane diverted to assist a reconnaissance team that was in enemy contact in the Khe Sanh area.

After aiding the team and being relieved by another aircraft, Byrd headed his plane back to Phu Bai. The weather was bad and the pilot reported at 1940 hours that he was lost and the weather worsening. The aircraft was not equipped to fly on instruments. Dong Ha and other radar controllers tried to get a fix on the Bird Dog and were able to maintain constant radio contact, but were able only to get an imprecise location. Based on the direction Byrd told them he was flying, the radar station advised him to climb because of mountains in the area. No further transmissions were heard.

Numerous searches were initiated following the disappearance of the aircraft, but were broken off after a few days due to weather conditions. When searches were resumed after the weather cleared, SAR failed to locate any wreckage. Capt. Byrd and 1Lt. O'Brien were declared **Missing In Action.**

O'BRIEN, KEVIN	BYRD, HUGH MCNEIL, JR.
Kevin O'Brien	Hugh McNeil Byrd, Jr.
Major/US Army	Captain/US Army
Headquarters & Headquarters Company,	220th Aviation Company, 212th Aviation Battalion, 1st Aviation Brigade Phu Bai Airfield, South Vietnam
2nd Battalion, 94th Artillery, 108th Artillery Group, Phu Bai Airfield, South Vietnam	22 October 1943 (Pueblo, CO)
30 August 1946 (Bronx, NY)	Berea, KY
Farmingville, NY	09 January 1969
09 January 1969	South Vietnam
South Vietnam	

Since the end of the Vietnam War there have been more than 21,000 reports received by our government about American prisoners, missing, and otherwise unaccounted for personnel. Many of these reports were from actual eye witnesses in the Southeast Asian theater and document LIVE Americans being held captive even today. How long will we allow this tragedy to continue?

American servicemen served selflessly and in harm's way in the decade long struggle in Southeast Asia to include Vietnam, Laos, Cambodia, and Thailand, were wounded, taken prisoner, and killed as witnessed by the 58,000 names on the black slab wall of remembrance in Washington D.C. Every missing fighting man who served in the Vietnam War deserves to be accounted for. America has always taken pride in leaving no fighting man behind. What can you do? Educate yourself on this subject.

Vietnam Journal
Valley of DEATH

SANCTUARY

SANCTUARY

LATE APRIL 1968, OPERATION DELAWARE. THE FIRST AIR CAVALRY, THE 101ST AIRBORNE DIVISION, AND ELEMENTS OF THE 196TH LIGHT INFANTRY BRIGADE PLUS THE ARVN FIRST DIVISION PUSHED HARD INTO THE A SHAU VALLEY.

THE MAKESHIFT OUTPOST WE WERE MANNING SEEMED SERIOUSLY UNDER PROTECTED, RELYING FAR TOO MUCH ON THE CHARITY OF THE MAIN UNITS UP AND DOWN THE VALLEY WHO, THEMSELVES, WERE UNDER CONSTANT HARRASSING PRESSURE FROM THE NVA ONLY A STONE'S THROW AWAY IN THEIR SANCTUARIES JUST ACROSS THE CAMBODIAN BORDER.

OR MAYBE THAT WAS WHY WE WERE VULNERABLE LOOKING AND APPARENTLY UNDER STRENGTH. THE PROVERBIAL CARROT ON A STICK THAT THE NVA JUST COULD NOT RESIST. PARANOIA WAS RAMPANT AND I WAS NOT IMMUNE.

IT WAS JUST AFTER DAWN WHEN SPECIAL FORCES SGT. WACO AND HIS TEAM APPEARED OUT OF THE MIST WITH HALF A DOZEN PRISONERS. IT APPEARED HE HAD BEEN RIGHT THE NIGHT BEFORE.

STORY & ART
DON LOMAX

I MUST ADMIT I WAS A LITTLE INTIMIDATED BY WACO. HE WAS A FIRECRACKER WITH THE FUSE LIT. AND IT APPEARED TO ME THAT HE PRETTY MUCH PLAYED BY HIS OWN RULES. I TRIED TO THINK OF SOME PLACE HE MIGHT FIT IN IN CIVILIAN LIFE BUT DREW A BLANK. THIS WAS HIS JOB AND HE WAS GOOD AT IT.

YOU'RE THAT WRITER GUY?

THAT'S RIGHT.

IT APPEARED I HAD CAUGHT HIM ON ONE OF HIS MORE MELLOW DAYS. PERHAPS HE HAD RELIEVED SOME PRESSURE OUT THERE DURING THE NIGHT. WHATEVER HAD HAPPENED OUT THERE I WOULD NOT HAVE WANTED TO BE ON THE RECEIVING END.

YOU BROUGHT SIX BACK ALIVE. HOW MANY DID YOU LEAVE IN PIECES OUT THERE?

ARE YOU THEIR UNION REP?

I HELD MY BREATH, REALIZING IT WAS A SMARTASS THING TO SAY AND EXPECTING HIM TO EXPLODE.

WE SENT THREE OF THE LITTLE MOTHER-FUCKERS TO BE WITH BUDDHA. THEY'RE PROBABLY SITTING IN THE FAT BASTARD'S LAP RIGHT NOW EATING THEIR FISH HEADS 'N' RICE AND THANKING ME FOR SENDING THEM TO BE WITH THEIR "ENLIGHTENED ONE".

I COULD NOT TELL IF THAT WAS SARCASM OR ENVY.

THAT NIGHT I DECIDED TO PRESS MY LUCK. I FOUND SGT. WACO'S HOLE AND INVITED MYSELF TO SQUAT WITH HIM FOR A WHILE UNTIL HE KICKED ME OUT.

DIP?

IS THAT A BRIBE?

ONLY IF IT'S WORKING

I'M ON MY THIRD TOUR AND I'VE SEEN A LOT OF SHITHEAD REPORTERS. MOST OF THEM EITHER DRUNK AT THE BAR IN THE CONTINENTAL HOTEL IN SAIGON OR DOWN ON TU DO STREET HUMPIN' THE BRAINS OUT OF SOME DINK HOOKER. BUT YOU'RE THE FIRST ONE WHO PUT HIS ASS IN THE GRASS WITH THE REST OF THE TROOPS.

THIS IS WHERE THE STORY IS.

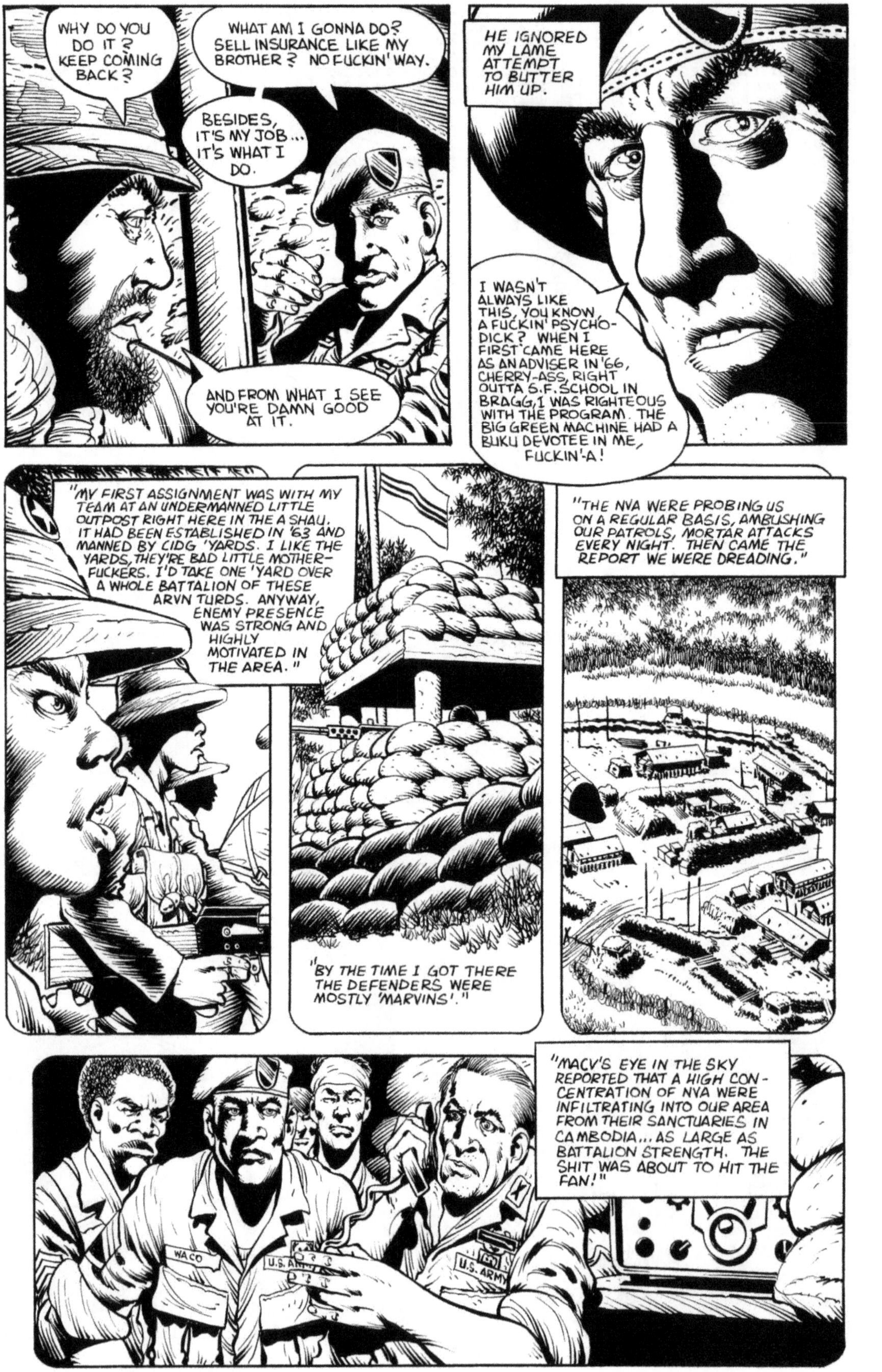
WHY DO YOU DO IT? KEEP COMING BACK?
WHAT AM I GONNA DO? SELL INSURANCE LIKE MY BROTHER? NO FUCKIN' WAY.
BESIDES, IT'S MY JOB... IT'S WHAT I DO.
AND FROM WHAT I SEE YOU'RE DAMN GOOD AT IT.
HE IGNORED MY LAME ATTEMPT TO BUTTER HIM UP.
I WASN'T ALWAYS LIKE THIS, YOU KNOW, A FUCKIN' PSYCHO-DICK? WHEN I FIRST CAME HERE AS AN ADVISER IN '66, CHERRY-ASS, RIGHT OUTTA S.F. SCHOOL IN BRAGG, I WAS RIGHTEOUS WITH THE PROGRAM. THE BIG GREEN MACHINE HAD A BUKU DEVOTEE IN ME, FUCKIN'-A!
"MY FIRST ASSIGNMENT WAS WITH MY TEAM AT AN UNDERMANNED LITTLE OUTPOST RIGHT HERE IN THE A SHAU. IT HAD BEEN ESTABLISHED IN '63 AND MANNED BY CIDG 'YARDS. I LIKE THE YARDS, THEY'RE BAD LITTLE MOTHER-FUCKERS. I'D TAKE ONE 'YARD OVER A WHOLE BATTALION OF THESE ARVN TURDS. ANYWAY, ENEMY PRESENCE WAS STRONG AND HIGHLY MOTIVATED IN THE AREA."
"BY THE TIME I GOT THERE THE DEFENDERS WERE MOSTLY 'MARVINS'."
"THE NVA WERE PROBING US ON A REGULAR BASIS, AMBUSHING OUR PATROLS, MORTAR ATTACKS EVERY NIGHT. THEN CAME THE REPORT WE WERE DREADING."
"MACV'S EYE IN THE SKY REPORTED THAT A HIGH CON-CENTRATION OF NVA WERE INFILTRATING INTO OUR AREA FROM THEIR SANCTUARIES IN CAMBODIA... AS LARGE AS BATTALION STRENGTH. THE SHIT WAS ABOUT TO HIT THE FAN!"
WACO
U.S. ARMY
U.S. ARMY

NERVES WERE FRAYED AS A DAMP FORBODING DARKNESS SETTLED ON THE PREVIOUSLY ABANDONED SPECIAL FORCES CAMP THAT THE 1ST OF THE 7TH NOW CALLED HOME.

CHIEU HOI, "OPEN ARMS", AN AMNESTY PROGRAM INSTITUTED IN 1963 WHERE ENEMY SOLDIERS, AFTER A SHORT REPATRIATION, WERE FORGIVEN THEIR SINS.

THE NUMBER OF AMNESTY SEEKERS BALLOONED AFTER THE ENEMY'S SOUND DEFEAT DURING THE TET OFFENSIVE EARLIER THIS YEAR.

CHIEU HOI SON OF A BITCH! I CAUGHT YOU! I KNOW YOUR GAME!

SGT. WACO, STAND DOWN!

I CAUGHT THE LITTLE BASTARD TOSSING ROCKS OVER THE WIRE! I KNOW HE HAS A SPOTTER OUT THERE IN THE BUSH!

TOSSING ROCKS?

HE THREW SIX LARGE ROCKS AND TWENTY THREE SMALL! HELL OF A COINCIDENCE THAT THAT NUMBER EXACTLY MATCHES OUR ARTILLERY PIECES AND MORTAR TUBES!

YOU'D BETTER CLEAN HOUSE, SGT. GARCIA! YOU'VE GOT INFILS IN YOUR OWN RANKS! CAREFUL, OR ONE OF THESE MORNINGS YOU'RE GONNA WAKE UP TOO DEAD TO ENJOY YOUR POWDERED EGGS FOR BREAKFAST!

YOU'RE GOING BACK OUT TONIGHT?

SOMEONE'S GOTTA CLEAN UP THIS MESS.

SO, DO YOU THINK HE'S RIGHT, OR IS HE LOSING IT?

PERSONALLY, I CAN'T STAND THE SON-OF-A-BITCH... BUT HE'S ONE HELL OF A SOLDIER. HE'S RIGHT. WE PROBABLY GOT MORE ENEMY INSIDE THE WIRE THAN OUTSIDE!

COMFORTING THOUGHT.

NIGHTY-NIGHT, JOURNAL.

"IT WAS MARCH '66, THE WEATHER WAS SHITTY, LIKE NOW, AND CPT. BOONE CANCELLED ALL PATROLS."

PULL IN ALL LISTENING POSTS, DOUBLE THE GUARDS ON THE PERIMETER, WE'LL HOLE UP AND WAIT THIS THING OUT. THE AIR FORCE HAS PROMISED MAX SUPPORT.

"WE HAD A 'YARD VILLE LESS THAN TWO KLICKS FROM OUT FRONT GATE. KNOWING THE ANIMOSITY BETWEEN THE VIETS AND THE MONTAGNARDS I KNEW WIPING OUT THEIR VILLAGE WOULD JUST SERVE AS AN APPETIZER WHILE ON THEIR WAY TO US."

DO WE BRING THE VILLAGERS IN?

"I WAS SHOCKED BY HIS ANSWER."

"NAÏVE AS I WAS, I THOUGHT WE WERE THERE TO HELP THE INDIGENOUS PEOPLE WITHSTAND THE COMMUNIST BLIGHT."

AND WHAT WOULD WE DO WITH THEM? WE DON'T HAVE THE ROOM OR FACILITIES. THEY'LL BE FINE.

NOW, DO WHAT I TOLD YOU, SERGEANT. IF YOU NEED ME I'LL BE IN THE COMMO BUNKER.

"I HAD NO DOUBT THAT IF WE AND THE 'YARDS SURVIVED THIS ACTION WE WOULD BE RIGHT BACK EXPECTING THEIR FULL COOPERATION AND LOYALTY WHEN IT WAS OVER. SUCH IS THE ARMY'S WARPED SENSE OF LOGIC. AND IF THE 'YARDS, WHO VALUE TRUTH AND LOYALTY, MIGHT HAVE THEIR NOSES A TAD OUT OF JOINT, COMMAND WILL, FOR THE LIFE OF THEM, BE UNABLE TO UNDERSTAND WHY."

"THERE WAS ONLY ONE MAN IN THE ENTIRE UNIT, OUTSIDE OF MY OWN A-TEAM, THAT I WOULD TRUST. I WOULD TRUST SIU, MY LIAISON, WITH MY LIFE, AND HAD ON SEVERAL OCCASIONS. I WAS A LITTLE EMBARRASSED TO FACE HIM BUT HE NEVER MENTIONED OUR ABANDONING HIS PEOPLE."

"WHEN IT CAME TO INSTINCT, INTUITION, AND SECOND SIGHT I HAD NEVER SEEN ANYONE HIS EQUAL. HE KNEW THE MOUNTAINS AROUND US. HE KNEW WHEN A BLADE OF GRASS WAS DISTURBED A KLICK AWAY. WHEN HE TOLD ME THERE WAS MOVEMENT IN THE TREELINE I DID NOT QUESTION IT."

"WE UNLOADED ON THE SPOT WITH M-79s..."

POM

POM

POM

"AND 81mm MORTARS!"

"IT FELT GOOD TO INITIATE FOR A CHANGE INSTEAD OF ALLOWING THE ENEMY TO PICK HIS OWN TIME FOR THE ATTACK THAT WE ALL KNEW WAS COMING! I IMAGINE IT WAS QUITE A SHOCK TO THE NVA."

POOT

POOT

"A BARRAGE OF H.E. LIT UP THE HILLSIDE."

BROOM

BROOM

TASTE IT, CHARLIE!

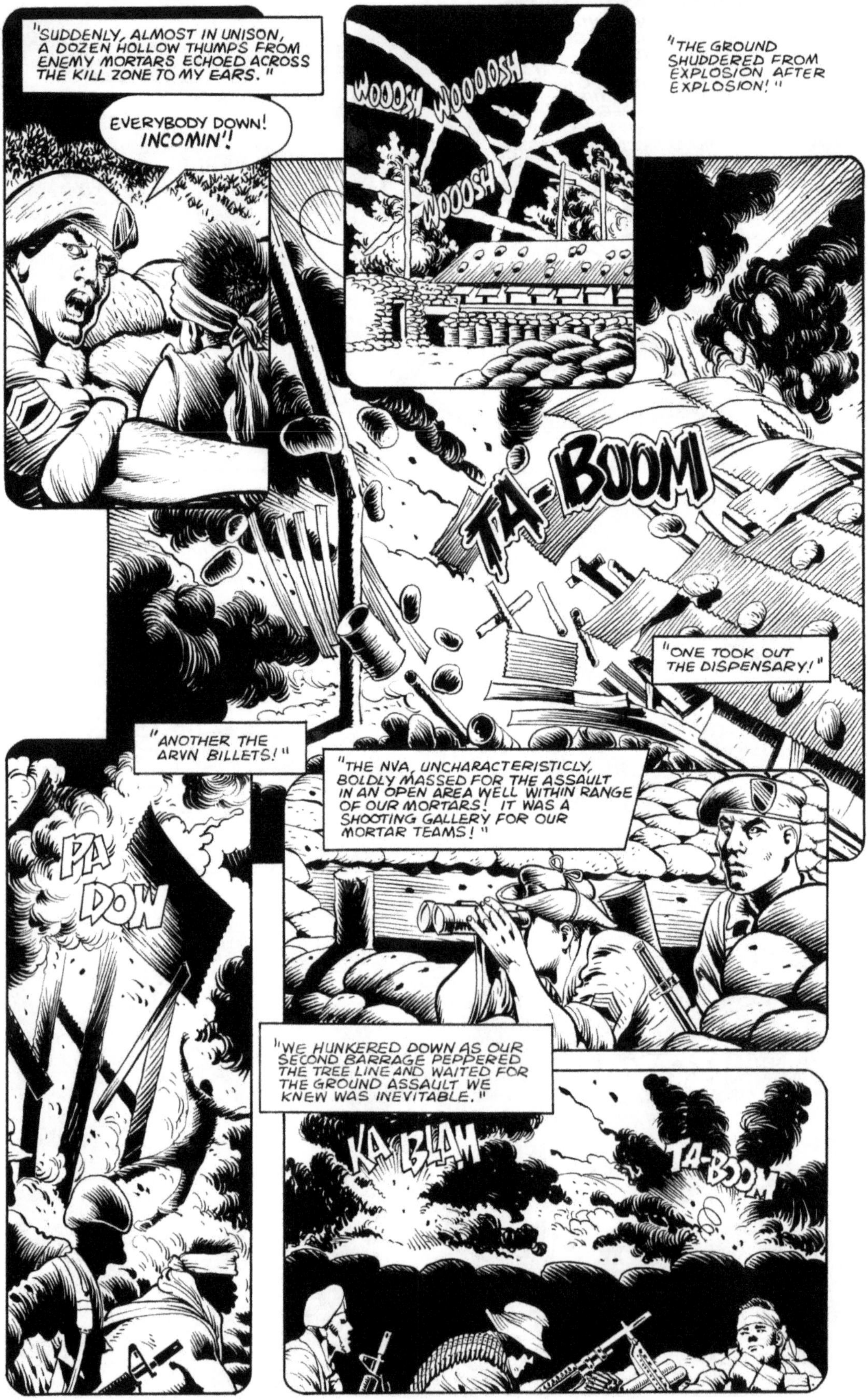
"SUDDENLY, ALMOST IN UNISON, A DOZEN HOLLOW THUMPS FROM ENEMY MORTARS ECHOED ACROSS THE KILL ZONE TO MY EARS."
EVERYBODY DOWN! INCOMIN'!
WOOOSH WOOOOOSH
WOOOSH
"THE GROUND SHUDDERED FROM EXPLOSION AFTER EXPLOSION!"
TA-BOOM
"ONE TOOK OUT THE DISPENSARY!"
"ANOTHER THE ARVN BILLETS!"
PA DOW
"THE NVA, UNCHARACTERISTICLY, BOLDLY MASSED FOR THE ASSAULT IN AN OPEN AREA WELL WITHIN RANGE OF OUR MORTARS! IT WAS A SHOOTING GALLERY FOR OUR MORTAR TEAMS!"
"WE HUNKERED DOWN AS OUR SECOND BARRAGE PEPPERED THE TREE LINE AND WAITED FOR THE GROUND ASSAULT WE KNEW WAS INEVITABLE."
KA BLAM
TA-BOOM

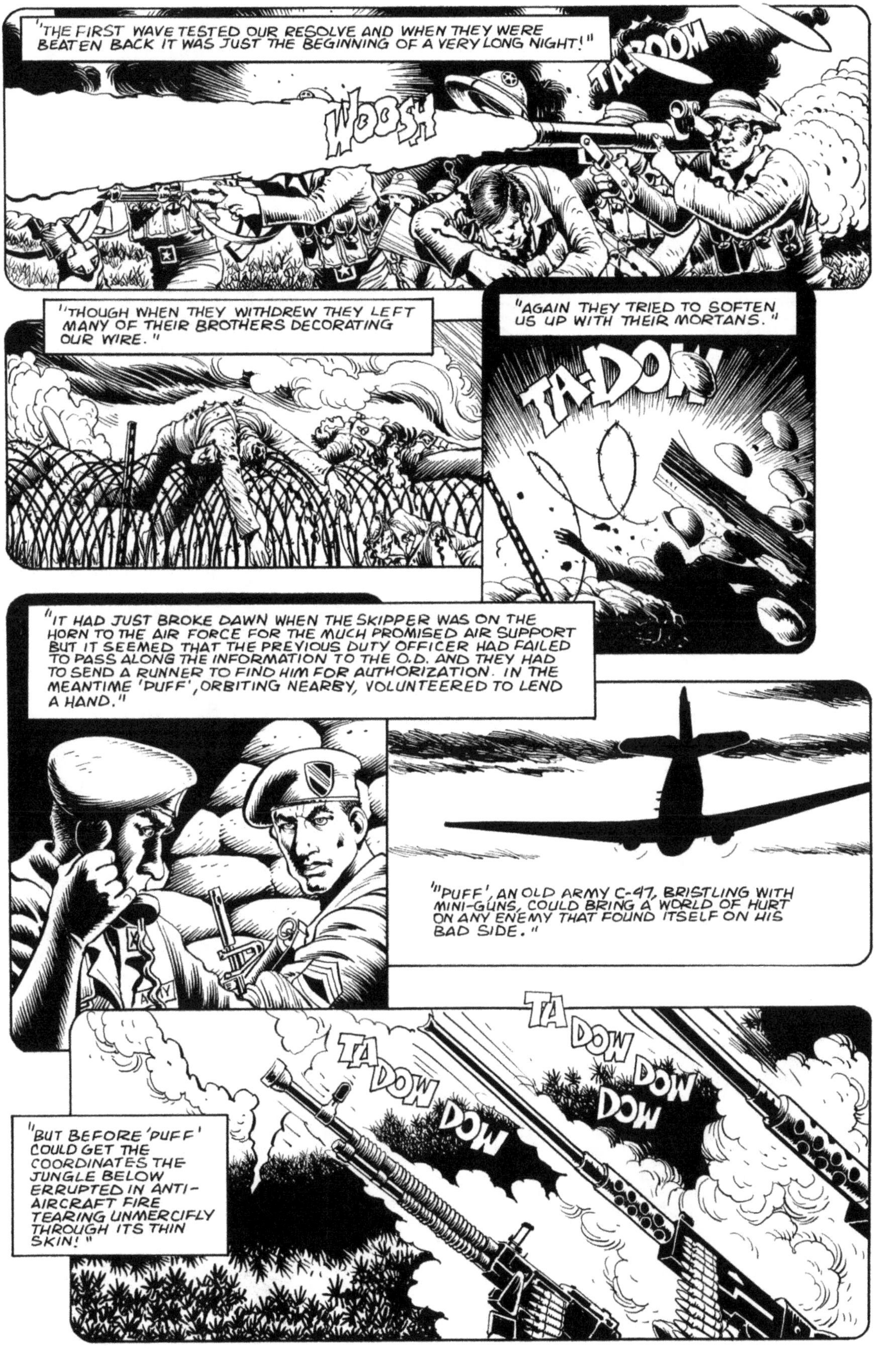
"THE FIRST WAVE TESTED OUR RESOLVE AND WHEN THEY WERE BEATEN BACK IT WAS JUST THE BEGINNING OF A VERY LONG NIGHT!"
TA-BOOM
WOOSH
"THOUGH WHEN THEY WITHDREW THEY LEFT MANY OF THEIR BROTHERS DECORATING OUR WIRE."
"AGAIN THEY TRIED TO SOFTEN US UP WITH THEIR MORTARS."
TA-DOW
"IT HAD JUST BROKE DAWN WHEN THE SKIPPER WAS ON THE HORN TO THE AIR FORCE FOR THE MUCH PROMISED AIR SUPPORT BUT IT SEEMED THAT THE PREVIOUS DUTY OFFICER HAD FAILED TO PASS ALONG THE INFORMATION TO THE O.D. AND THEY HAD TO SEND A RUNNER TO FIND HIM FOR AUTHORIZATION. IN THE MEANTIME 'PUFF', ORBITING NEARBY, VOLUNTEERED TO LEND A HAND."
"'PUFF', AN OLD ARMY C-47, BRISTLING WITH MINI-GUNS, COULD BRING A WORLD OF HURT ON ANY ENEMY THAT FOUND ITSELF ON HIS BAD SIDE."
TA DOW DOW DOW
TA DOW DOW
"BUT BEFORE 'PUFF' COULD GET THE COORDINATES THE JUNGLE BELOW ERRUPTED IN ANTI-AIRCRAFT FIRE TEARING UNMERCIFLY THROUGH ITS THIN SKIN!"

"THEN THE SKY FILLED WITH B-40 ROCKET TRAILS. THE NVA HAD THEIR SHIT TOGETHER TIME!"

"WE HEARD THE EXPLOSION THAT BROUGHT HIM DOWN. A MUFFLED THUMP, THEN THE SPUTTERING ENGINE. NOT A GOOD SIGN."

"THEY SAY HE BURNED IN FROM ALTITUDE PLOWING A FURROW A HUNDRED YARDS IN THE THICKLY MATTED JUNGLE RIGHT THROUGH THE NVA STAGING AREA."

"THE CREW WAS NEVER ACCOUNTED FOR. WHETHER THE JUNGLE GOT THEM OR THE NVA, I NEVER HEARD."

"THEN, LIKE GHOSTS OUT OF THE MIST, A PAIR OF SKYRAIDERS CHURNED UP THE VALLEY LOADED FOR BEAR! WE NOW HAD THE NAVY INVOLVED BUT STILL NO SIGN OF THE AIR FORCE. THE PAIR OF A-1Hs SCREAMED PAST OUR POSITION SO CLOSE WE COULD SEE THE DETERMINED LOOK ON THE PILOT'S FACES."

"THEY DROPPED THEIR PAYLOAD RIGHT ON THE MARK WITHOUT ANY PROMPTING FROM US. THEY MUST HAVE HAD AN FAC IN THE NEIGHBORHOOD THAT WE HAD NOT SEEN. NOT SURPRISING, WITH THE CEILING AS LOW AS IT WAS."

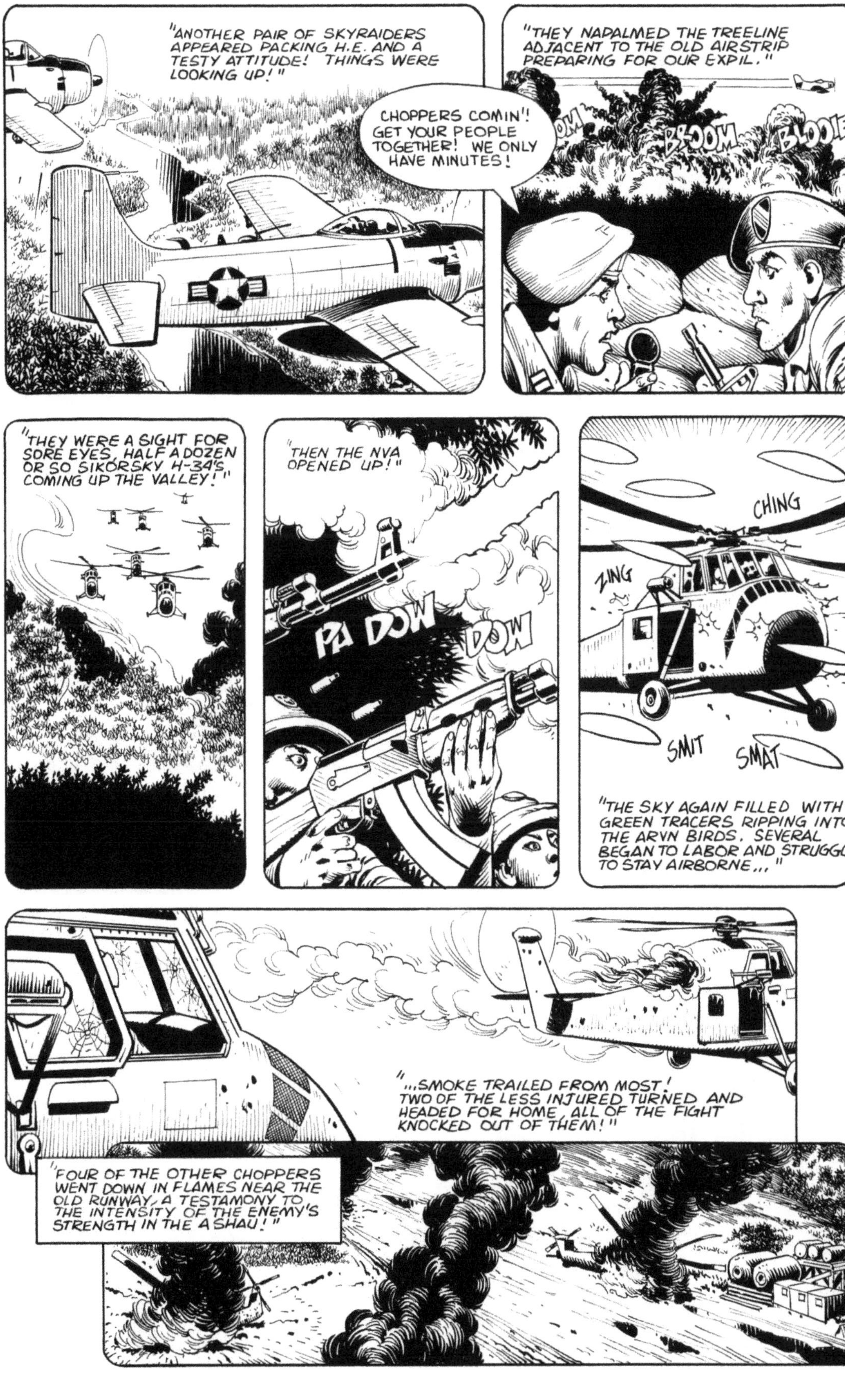
"ANOTHER PAIR OF SKYRAIDERS APPEARED PACKING H.E. AND A TESTY ATTITUDE! THINGS WERE LOOKING UP!"
CHOPPERS COMIN'! GET YOUR PEOPLE TOGETHER! WE ONLY HAVE MINUTES!
"THEY NAPALMED THE TREELINE ADJACENT TO THE OLD AIRSTRIP PREPARING FOR OUR EXFIL."
B'OOM
BLOOIE
"THEY WERE A SIGHT FOR SORE EYES, HALF A DOZEN OR SO SIKORSKY H-34'S, COMING UP THE VALLEY!"
"THEN THE NVA OPENED UP!"
PA DOW
DOW
CHING
ZING
SMIT
SMAT
"THE SKY AGAIN FILLED WITH GREEN TRACERS RIPPING INTO THE ARVN BIRDS. SEVERAL BEGAN TO LABOR AND STRUGGLE TO STAY AIRBORNE..."
"...SMOKE TRAILED FROM MOST! TWO OF THE LESS INJURED TURNED AND HEADED FOR HOME, ALL OF THE FIGHT KNOCKED OUT OF THEM!"
"FOUR OF THE OTHER CHOPPERS WENT DOWN IN FLAMES NEAR THE OLD RUNWAY, A TESTAMONY TO THE INTENSITY OF THE ENEMY'S STRENGTH IN THE A SHAU!"

"I THINK IT WAS THE FIRST PAIR OF SKYRAIDERS, REFITTED AND BACK FOR A SECOND BOMBING RUN, THAT DREW THE NVA'S MURDEROUS ATTENTION."

KA DU DU DU DU

"THE WALL OF LEAD TURNED THE LEAD A-1H'S TAIL SECTION INTO SWISS CHEESE. FROM THAT MOMENT ON HIS FATE WAS SEALED."

CHING

CLANG

KLING

"IT WAS A MIRACLE THAT THE PILOT WAS ABLE TO KEEP THE WOUNDED BIRD ALOFT LONG ENOUGH TO CLEAR THE TREES AND CRASH LAND AT THE FAR END OF THE OLD RUNWAY."

"THE LANDING WAS ROUGH WHEN THE LANDING GEAR COLLAPSED BUT THE PILOT, COMMANDER VINCE TAYLOR OF HUNINGTON BEACH, CA, MANAGED TO CRAWL OUT OF THE FLAMING AIRCRAFT. HE TOOK COVER IN A DRAINAGE DITCH TO PLAN HIS NEXT MOVE."

"CDR TAYLOR'S WINGMAN, LTJG OWEN PINSKI, WAS NOT ABOUT TO LET THAT HAPPEN!"

"WHATEVER WAS TO BE DONE HAD TO BE DONE THAT MOMENT AS A DOZEN NVA BROKE COVER AND CHARGED HIS POSITION. CAPTURING OR KILLING AN AMERICAN FLIER WAS HIGH ON THE LIST OF DESIRABLES FOR THE AVERAGE NVA."

TA DOW DOW DOW

"THERE WAS A STANDING REWARD AND A PROMISE OF ADVANCEMENT PROMISED BY THE NORTH VIETNAMESE POLITBURO."

"REPEATED STRAFFING RUNS GAVE THE NVA SOMETHING ELSE TO THINK ABOUT. BY THE THIRD RUN THE NVA SURVIVORS HAD SCURRIED BACK TO THE COVER OF THE THICK JUNGLE."

BBBBBBBRRAP

"IT WOULD BE TOUCH AND GO!"

"LTJG PINSKI ROLLED TO A STOP, HIS ENGINE REVVING TO GET CDR TAYLOR'S ATTENTION"

"CDR TAYLOR DID NOT NEED AN INVITATION. HE WAS ALREADY APPROACHING AT A DEAD RUN!"

TA DOW DOW   PA DOW DOW

"LTJG PINSKI'S SKYRAIDER WAS ALREADY ROLLING AS CDR TAYLOR DOVE HEAD FIRST INTO HIS WINGMAN'S LAP!"

SMAT   SMT   SMT

"PINSKI SLAMMED THE THROTTLE TO THE FIREWALL AND THE BIG R-3350 CYCLONE ENGINE CHEWED ITS WAY INTO THE SKY TO RETURN TO THE USS INTREPID WITH A HARROWING STORY TO TELL!"

VROOOOM

"AGAIN, WE WERE HIT HARD BY NVA MORTARS..."

BROOOM

"...AND B-40 ROCKETS! THIS INTENSE 'SOFTENING UP' COULD ONLY MEAN ONE THING..."

THA-ROOM

WOOOSH

WOOOSH

WOOOSH

BA-DA-DAP

BA-BA-BAP

TA DOW DOW

"...MASS ASSAULT ON THE COMPOUND! THE FIRST WAVE HIT US AROUND 0330."

"THEIR LOSSES WERE STAGGERING..."

"AND STILL THEY KEPT COMING..."

"...STEPPING ON THE BODIES OF THEIR FALLEN COMRADES TO BREACH OUR WIRE!"

"ARVN MOMMA-SAN'S BOYS WHO WERE SUPPOSE TO DEFEND THE PERIMETER COLLAPSED. DICIPLINE WENT OUT THE WINDOW. THEY WERE LEFT SOBBING LIKE BABIES, BEGGING FOR MERCY WITH THEIR LITTLE HANDS IN THE AIR!"

"A LOT OF GOOD IT DID THEM. MOST WERE EXECUTED ON THE SPOT. CHARLIE DON'T LIKE CRYBABIES. I TOOK COMMAND OF THE REMAINING ARVN WITH LITTLE PROTEST FROM THEIR INDECISIVE OFFICERS AND NCOs. WE FELL BACK TO OUR FINAL LINE OF DEFENSE, THE COMMO BUNKER."

"THE NVA CHARGED AGAIN,..."

"AND WE BEAT THE BACK, PROVING THAT THEY COULD DO IT WITH WELL DICIPLINED FIRE AND CONFIDENCE IN THE INDIVIDUAL LEADING THEM."

"IT MAY SEEM TO YOU THAT I'M PAINTING ALL ARVN WITH A BROAD BRUSH, BUT THAT'S NOT TRUE. I'VE SEEN INDIVIDUAL BRAVERY, JUST NEVER IN THEIR CHAIN OF COMMAND."

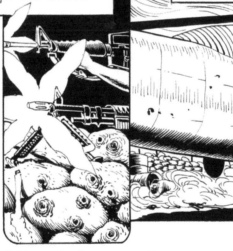

"LIKE THE H-3A PILOT WITH BALLS THE SIZE OF WATERMELONS... LANDING HIS RICKETY OLD CHOPPER NOT 20 METERS FROM OUR LOCATION!"

"I DID THE BEST I COULD TO CALM THE PANICKED ARVN. WE LOADED THE WOUNDED FIRST... BUT I KNEW WE WERE ONLY A HEARTBEAT FROM CHAOS!"

"LIKE THE SNAPPING OF A TWIG THEY ALL TURNED INTO AN ANGRY MOB, CHARGING THE CHOPPER, TEARING EACH OTHER APART TO GET A SEAT ON, WHAT THEY THOUGHT WAS THE ONLY TICKET IN TOWN!"

"I WAS FORCED TO FIRE OVER THEIR HEADS TO DRIVE THEM BACK OR THE CHOPPER WOULD HAVE NEVER GOTTEN OFF THE GROUND!"

"WE GOT THE WOUNDED LOADED AND THE ARVN PILOT REPORTED THAT AMERICAN CHOPPERS WERE INBOUND TO GET THE REST OF US! I COULDA KISSED HIM, AND I AIN'T YOU KNOW... LIKE THAT."

"BUT OUR RESCUERS WERE HAVING A HARD TIME OF IT THEMSELVES! THE RADIO CRACKLED, 'WE'VE BEEN HIT! WE'RE GOING IN... REPEAT, WE'RE——,' THEN SILENCE. WE ALL KNEW WHAT THAT MEANT."

BROOOM

"WITH THE NVA REGROUPING, I DECIDED TO TAKE THE OPPORTUNITY TO RELOCATE AT THE OLD AIRSTRIP. A MORE REASONABLE LOCATION FOR EXFIL."

"OUR RESCUERS NEEDED RESCUED."

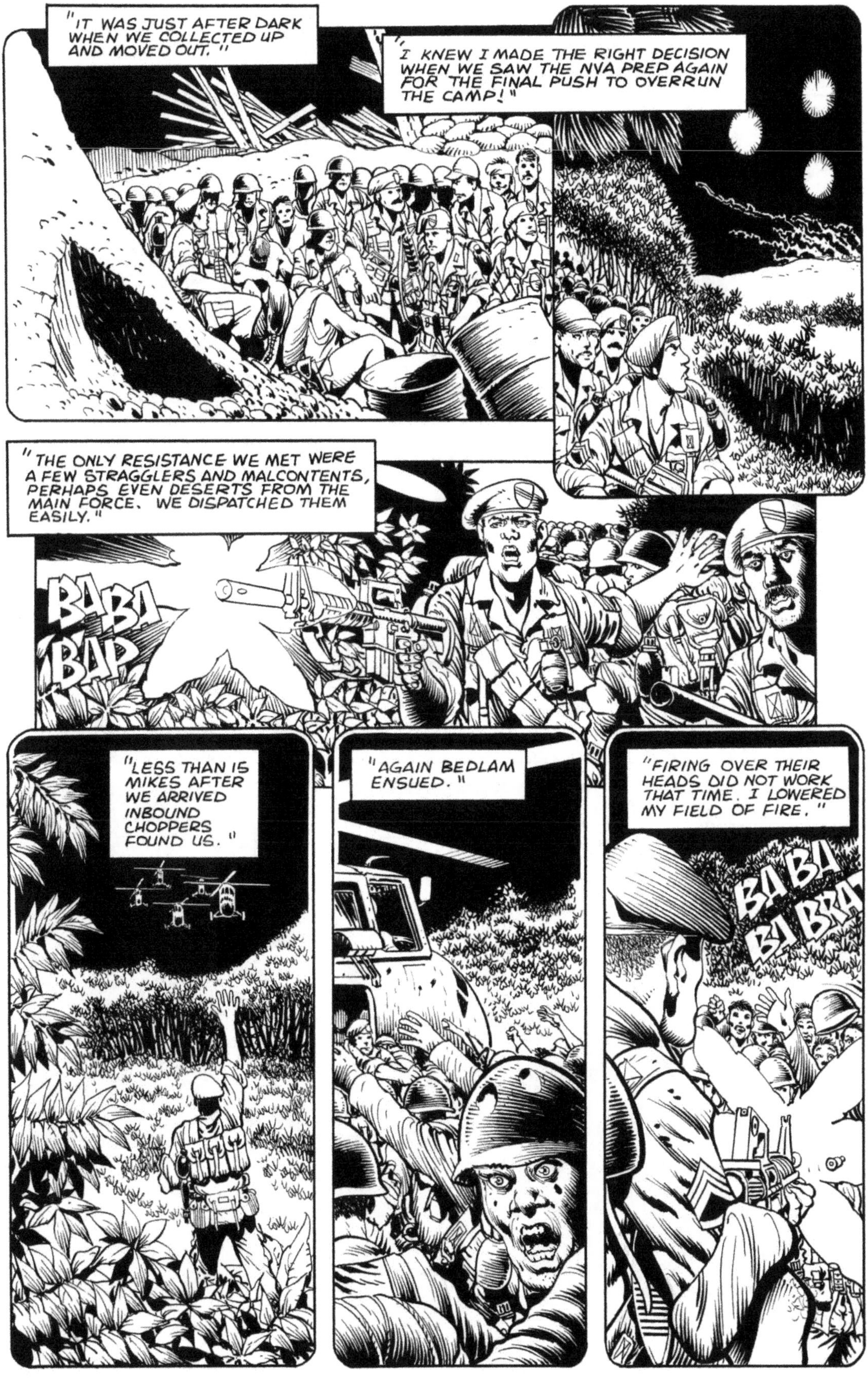
"IT WAS JUST AFTER DARK WHEN WE COLLECTED UP AND MOVED OUT."
"I KNEW I MADE THE RIGHT DECISION WHEN WE SAW THE NVA PREP AGAIN FOR THE FINAL PUSH TO OVERRUN THE CAMP!"
"THE ONLY RESISTANCE WE MET WERE A FEW STRAGGLERS AND MALCONTENTS, PERHAPS EVEN DESERTS FROM THE MAIN FORCE. WE DISPATCHED THEM EASILY."
BABA
BAP
"LESS THAN 15 MIKES AFTER WE ARRIVED INBOUND CHOPPERS FOUND US."
"AGAIN BEDLAM ENSUED."
"FIRING OVER THEIR HEADS DID NOT WORK THAT TIME. I LOWERED MY FIELD OF FIRE."
BA BA
BA BRAT

"WE LOADED THE REST OF THE WOUNDED ON THE FIRST BIRD, THEN AS MANY OF THE ARVN AS POSSIBLE ON THE REST OF THE CHOPPERS."

"MY TEAM AND I TOOK THE LAST TAXI IN THAT WAVE WITH A GUARANTEE FROM MACV THAT THERE WERE MORE INBOUND TO SNAG THE REST."

"I DID MY BEST TO WARN THEM THAT THE SITUATION WAS DIRE AND THAT DICIPLINE AT THE EVAC SITE WAS NONEXISTENT."

"THEY TOO WERE CHARGED BY THE PANICKED MOB AND WOULD PROBABLY HAVE BEEN SWAMPED BY THE HORDE EXCEPT THAT..."

"IT WAS ABOUT THAT TIME WHEN NVA MORTARS ZEROED IN ON THE LZ AND DEALT A LITTLE CROWD CONTROL OF THEIR OWN."

"THE AIR FORCE NEVER DID SHOW UP."

AND THAT IS WHY I HAVE LITTLE USE FOR "MARVIN THE ARVN", AND EVEN LESS FOR THE AIR FORCE.

WHAT HAPPENED TO THE FIREBASE?

AS FAR AS I KNOW THE NVA TURNED IT INTO A SUPPLY AND R&R DEPOT. THAT'S WHAT I WOULD DO WITH ITS CLOSE PROXIMITY TO THE HO CHI MINH TRAIL.

YOU'LL BE ABLE TO FIND OUT FIRST HAND. WORD IS WE'RE GOING BACK, DEAL A LITTLE KARMA TO NATHIENAL VICTOR! ABOUT GODDAMN TIME!

DAWN FOUND US HUMPIN' IT UP THE VALLEY THROUGH CENTURIES OLD VEGETATION. I TRIED TO IMAGINE THE FRENCH DECADES BEFORE PATROLLING THE SAME TRAILS AND FACING THE SAME DETERMINED ENEMY WE WERE FACING. IT IS ABSOLUTELY TRUE, WAR IS ETERNAL.

CONVERSATION WITH SGT. WACO SUDDENLY DRIED UP. A GOOD REPORTER KNOWS WHEN TO SHUT THE HELL UP. THIS WAS JUST ONE OF THOSE TIMES. I DIDN'T WANT T WEAR OUT MY WELCOME.

BY MIDDAY WE FOUND AND CLEARED ANOTHER CIDG CAMP WITH NO RESISTANCE. THE NVA HAD APPARENTLY DESERTED IT AND FLED BACK INTO CAMBODIA. I HOPED THAT THE SAME WAS IN STORE FOR US AT SGT. WACO'S FORMER FIREBASE.

WE LEFT A SMALL DETACHMENT AT THE CAMP AND PRESSED ON. THE WEATHER WAS DAMP AND THERE WAS AN UNCHARACTERISTIC CHILL IN THE AIR. EVEN SO I WAS SWEATING... THAT COLD FORBODING SWEAT. THE JUNGLE WAS GETTING TO ME.

WE STUMBLED ONTO A WELL USED CORDUROY ROAD THAT THE ENEMY WAS OBVIOUSLY USING TO INFILTRATE SUPPLIES FROM THE HO CHI MINH TRAIL.

THE TREES ON BOTH SIDES WERE PULLED TOGETHER AT THE TOP AND SECURED TO GUARD FROM PRYING EYES FROM ABOVE. IT GAVE THE PLACE A FEELING OF REVERENCE, ALMOST CHAPEL-LIKE.

TA-BOOOM

I WAS SNAPPED BACK TO REALITY BY THE BONE-JARRING REPORT OF A BROKEN DOWN T-54 TANK'S MAIN GUN THAT THE NVA WERE USING FOR SECURITY AT THE SITE!

BECAUSE OF THE HEAVY UNDERGROWTH, THE ENEMY TANKERS COULD NOT TRAVERSE THE TURRET RIGHT OR LEFT. THE CAVALRY TROOPERS PICKED UP ON THAT FACT QUICKLY AND THEY BROKE OUT THE LAW ROCKETS TO ATTACK THE MAKESHIFT GUN EMPLACEMENT FROM ITS FLANK.

WOOOSH!

THE FIRST ROCKET DISABLED THE MAIN CANNON.

CLANG

THE SECOND TOUCHED OFF THE POWDER MAGAZINE, END OF STORY.

BOO

WE CAUGHT THE OCCUPANTS OF SGT. WACO'S FORMER FIREBASE WITH THEIR PANTS DOWN. THEY WERE MOSTLY LOWER ECHELON COOKS, MECHANICS, AND MEDICAL PERSONNEL.

THE FIGHT WAS SHORT AND BRUTAL!

WHILE THE TROOPS WERE MOPPING UP I FOUND WHAT SGT. WACO HAD DESCRIBED AS THE COMMO BUNKER. THE NVA WERE APPARENTLY USING IT AS A DISPENSARY. THERE WAS BLOOD EVERYWHERE ATTESTING TO THE INTENSITY OF THE OPERATIONS AGAINST US.

THE TROOPS COLLECTED ALL OF THE ENEMY WEAPONS AND AMMO AND BLEW IT IN PLACE BEFORE RETURNING TO THE FIGHT.

TA-BOOM

OUT BACK WE FOUND A HUGE PILE OF AMPUTATED, DAMMAGED LIMBS. THE FIRST CAV WAS OBVIOUSLY LEAVING A MARK.

I NEVER SAW SGT. WACO AFTER THE OPERATION BUT I HAD A FEELING HE WAS SPORTING A TREMENDOUS SHIT EATING GRIN. EVEN IF THE NVA WERE TO MOVE RIGHT BACK IN THE MINUTE WE MOVED ON. THE PAYBACK WAS SWEET FOR HIM, I AM SURE.

NEXT:
the ENEMY

Missing American

Lt. Col. Norman M. Green and 1Lt.Wayne C. Irsch shot down in Laos and MIA since 1968

The following profiles two of those Missing Americans:

Lt. Col. Norman M. Green and 1Lt. Wayne C. Irsch were piloting an F4 Phantom in Vietnam. The Phantom represented the ultimate fighter plane and was one of the most sought after assignments for pilots.

On January 9, 1968, Green and Irsch were assigned a combat mission which took them over Laos. It was Irsch's job to operate much of the high-tech equipment on the aircraft. When near the city of Sepone in Savannaklet Province of Laos, their aircraft was hit by enemy fire and crashed. Their loss location is listed as 40 miles south-southeast of the Ban Karai Pass. Both men were classified as **Missing In Action.**

On September 13, 1968, a statement by Soth Pethrasi was monitored from Puerto Rico in which the names of several Americans were mentioned. The report stated that "Smith, Christiano, Jeffords, and Mauterer" were part of "several dozen captured Airmen" whom the Pathet Lao were "treating correctly and who were still in Laos. Another name, Norman Morgan, captured January 9, 1968 was mentioned but is not on lists of missing. This is believed to possible correlate to Norman Green.

The Ban Karai Pass, on the border of Vietnam and Laos, is an area which claimed many pilots during the war in Indochina. Many of the pilots were able to safely reach the ground, but were not released at the end of the war. Although the Pathet Lao stated publicly many times that they held prisoners that would be released only from Laos, the U.S. did not include Laos in the agreement ending the American involvement in the war. Not a single American Military prisoner of war in Laos has been released.

GREEN, NORMAN MORGAN

Norman Morgan Green
Colonel/US Air Force
497th Tactical Fighter Squadron

Ubon Airbase, Thailand
16 July 1923
Washington, DC
09 January 1968
Laos

IRSCH, WAYNE CHARLES

Wayne Charles Irsch
Captain/US Air Force
497th Tactical Fighter Squadron

Ubon Airbase, Thailand
25 April 1942
Tulsa, OK
09 January 1968
Laos

Since the end of the Vietnam War there have been more than 21,000 reports received by our government about American prisoners, missing, and otherwise unaccounted for personnel. Many of these reports were from actual eye witnesses in the Southeast Asian theater and document LIVE Americans being held captive even today. How long will we allow this tragedy to continue?

American servicemen served selflessly and in harm's way in the decade long struggle in Southeast Asia to include Vietnam, Laos, Cambodia, and Thailand, were wounded, taken prisoner, and killed as witnessed by the 58,000 names on the black slab wall of remembrance in Washington D.C. Every missing fighting man who served in the Vietnam War deserves to be accounted for. America has always taken pride in leaving no fighting man behind. What can you do? Educate yourself on this subject.

Vietnam Journal
Valley of DEATH

THE ENEMY

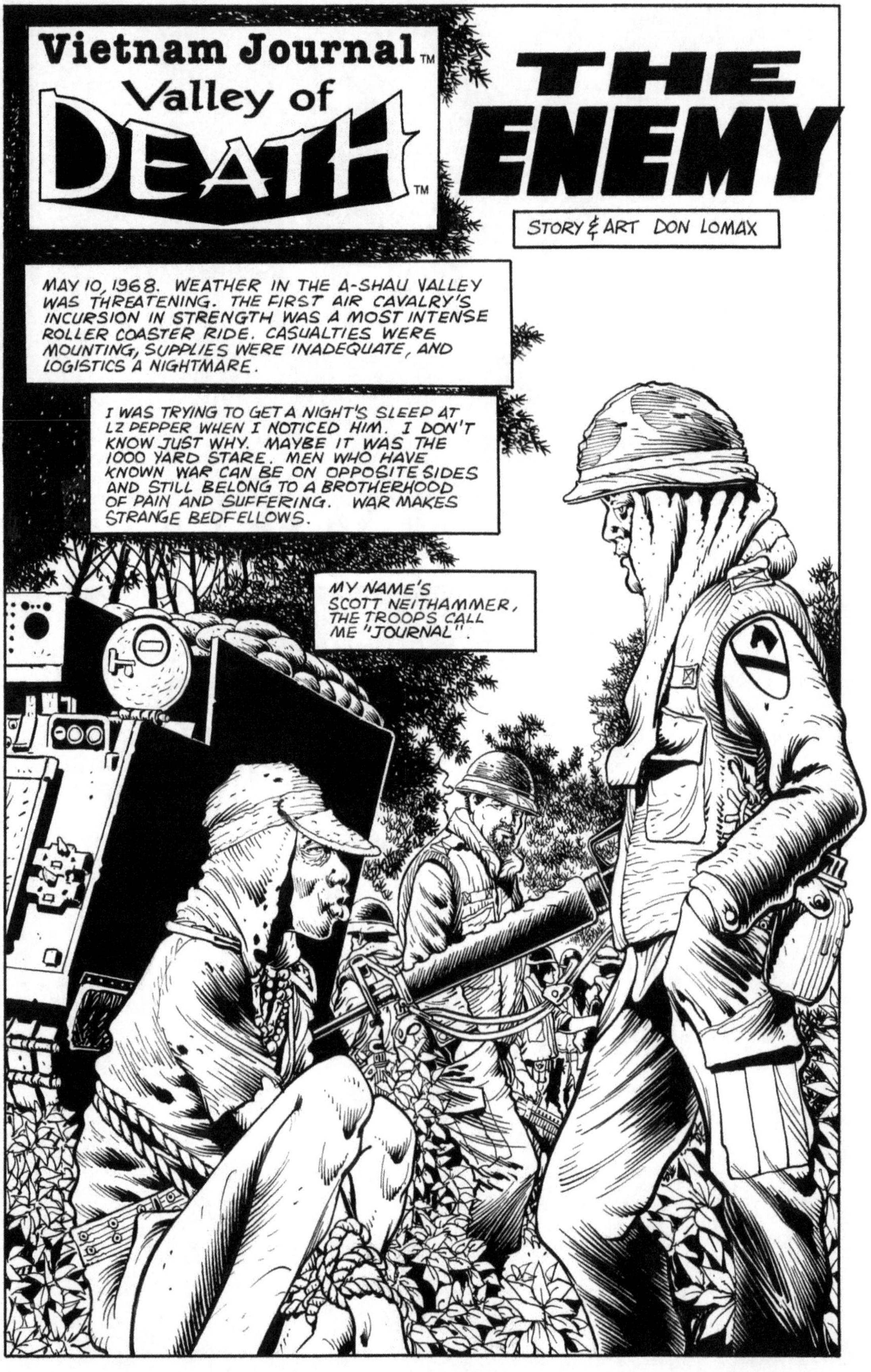
Vietnam Journal™
Valley of DEATH™
THE ENEMY
STORY & ART DON LOMAX
MAY 10, 1968. WEATHER IN THE A-SHAU VALLEY WAS THREATENING. THE FIRST AIR CAVALRY'S INCURSION IN STRENGTH WAS A MOST INTENSE ROLLER COASTER RIDE. CASUALTIES WERE MOUNTING, SUPPLIES WERE INADEQUATE, AND LOGISTICS A NIGHTMARE.
I WAS TRYING TO GET A NIGHT'S SLEEP AT LZ PEPPER WHEN I NOTICED HIM. I DON'T KNOW JUST WHY. MAYBE IT WAS THE 1000 YARD STARE. MEN WHO HAVE KNOWN WAR CAN BE ON OPPOSITE SIDES AND STILL BELONG TO A BROTHERHOOD OF PAIN AND SUFFERING. WAR MAKES STRANGE BEDFELLOWS.
MY NAME'S SCOTT NEITHAMMER, THE TROOPS CALL ME "JOURNAL".

HE WAS JUST ONE OF DOZENS, NO... HUNDREDS OF PRISONERS THAT I HAD STUMBLED ACROSS BEING HELD BY ARVN OR U.S. TROOPS DURING THIS EXTENSIVE OPERATION.

I DO NOT KNOW WHY HE CAUGHT MY ATTENTION. HE WAS JUST ANOTHER PRISONER. MAYBE BECAUSE OF THE ALMOST COMICAL JUMBLE OF CLOTHING AND EQUIPMENT HE CARRIED. A TRUE ANOMALY.

THE INTERPRETER WAS A KIT CARSON SCOUT NAMED HUNG, AN INDIVIDUAL I HAD VISITED EARLIER IN THE DAY AND WHEN I SAW HIM WITH THE PRISONER...

HUNG... WHAT'S THIS GUY'S STORY?

JOURNAL-SAN. YOU GOT A SMOKE?

I FIND CIGARETTES A GOOD WAY TO BREAK THE ICE WITH THE AVERAGE GRUNT OR LOCAL. THOUGH I DO NOT SMOKE MYSELF I HAVE TAKEN TO CARRYING AS A CATALYST TO PUT THOSE I INTERVIEW MORE AT EASE. TRICKS OF THE TRADE.

SURE.

MUCH OBLIGED.

I WAITED. HUNG WAS NOT ONE TO BE RUSHED.

HE IS PACOH. PACOHS ARE ONLY MONTAGNARD TRIBE IN THE A SHAU.

TOUGH LITTLE MOTHER-FUCKERS, YA KNOW?

I KNEW. OF THE 33 MONTAGNARD TRIBES OF SOUTH VIETNAM ONLY THE PACOHS WERE HARDY ENOUGH TO CALL THE A SHAU HOME. DARK FORBODING RAIN FORESTS AND CONTINUALLY INCLEMENT WEATHER, THE A SHAU HAD BEEN THEIR HOME FOR THOUSANDS OF YEARS. THEY KNEW NOTHING ELSE.

WHAT'S HE SAY?

SAYS HE JUST WANTS TO BE LEFT ALONE.

DON'T WE ALL?

HOW MUCH DO YOU WANNA HEAR, JOURNAL-SAN?

ALL OF IT... I GOT NOTHIN' ELSE TO DO.

HE HAS SPOKE OF HIS CHILDHOOD. HE SPOKE OF HIS ANCESTORS. FOR MORE THAN TWO HUNDRED YEARS HIS PEOPLE LIVED AT PEACE IN THE VALLEY.

"WHEN HE WAS A YOUNGSTER HIS FAMILY, HIS TRIBE, GOT EVERYTHING THEY NEEDED FROM THE VALLEY."

"THEY LIVED A QUIET, SHY LIFE PROTECTED FROM THE OUTSIDE WORLD BY THE MOUNTAINS, SHELTERED BY THOUSAND-YEAR-OLD TREES IN A LUSH GARDEN OF EDEN THAT PROVIDED THEIR EVERY NEED."

"THEY GREW THEIR OWN VEGETABLES, FRUIT, RICE, EVEN TOBACCO."

"FRUITS, NUTS, BERRIES, BAMBOO SHOOTS..."

"EVERYTHING THEY NEEDED FOR A COMPLETE, HAPPY LIFE."

"THE FOREST PROVIDED MEAT..."

"THOUGH THEY HAVE NO WRITTEN LANGUAGE THE STORY TELLERS AND HOLY MEN KEPT THEIR HISTORY ALIVE AROUND THE FIRES. IT WAS A MELLOW, FULFILLING CHILDHOOD OF NEVERENDING FEASTS AND CELEBRATIONS."

"THEY WERE NOT IGNORANT OF THE OUTSIDE WORLD. THEY SIMPLY CHOSE NOT TO ACKNOWLEDGE IT EXISTED."

"NEVERENDING, AT LEAST IN HIS YOUNG EYES."

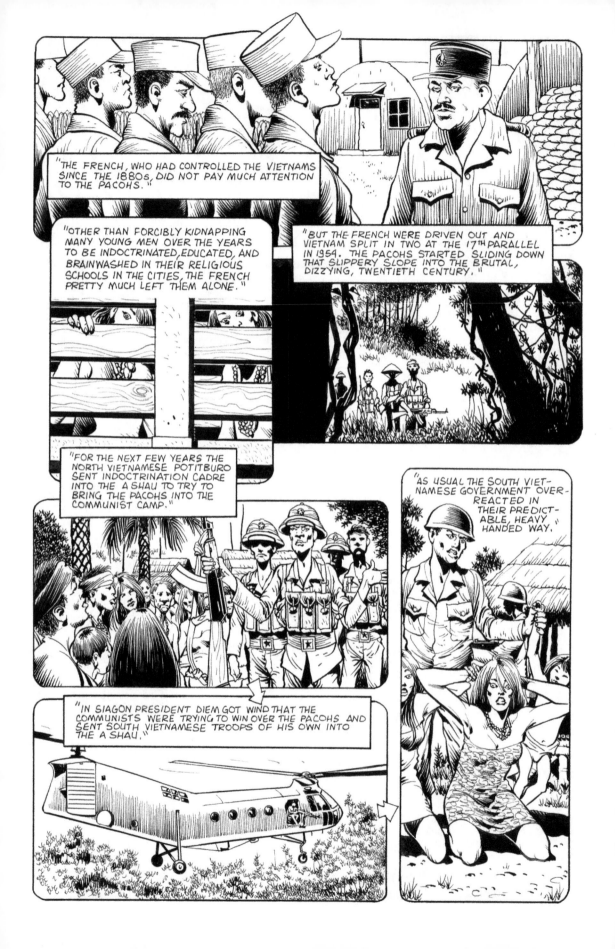

"THE FRENCH, WHO HAD CONTROLLED THE VIETNAMS SINCE THE 1880s, DID NOT PAY MUCH ATTENTION TO THE PACOHS."

"OTHER THAN FORCIBLY KIDNAPPING MANY YOUNG MEN OVER THE YEARS TO BE INDOCTRINATED, EDUCATED, AND BRAINWASHED IN THEIR RELIGIOUS SCHOOLS IN THE CITIES, THE FRENCH PRETTY MUCH LEFT THEM ALONE."

"BUT THE FRENCH WERE DRIVEN OUT AND VIETNAM SPLIT IN TWO AT THE 17TH PARALLEL IN 1954. THE PACOHS STARTED SLIDING DOWN THAT SLIPPERY SLOPE INTO THE BRUTAL, DIZZYING, TWENTIETH CENTURY."

"FOR THE NEXT FEW YEARS THE NORTH VIETNAMESE POTITBURO SENT INDOCTRINATION CADRE INTO THE A SHAU TO TRY TO BRING THE PACOHS INTO THE COMMUNIST CAMP."

"AS USUAL THE SOUTH VIET-NAMESE GOVERNMENT OVER-REACTED IN THEIR PREDICT-ABLE, HEAVY HANDED WAY."

"IN SIAGON PRESIDENT DIEM GOT WIND THAT THE COMMUNISTS WERE TRYING TO WIN OVER THE PACOHS AND SENT SOUTH VIETNAMESE TROOPS OF HIS OWN INTO THE A SHAU."

"PRESIDENT DIEM ORDERED ALL OF THE MONTAGNARDS IN NORTHERN I CORPS TO LEAVE THEIR VILLAGES AND MOVE TO THE COASTAL CITIES WHERE THE SIAGON GOVERNMENT COULD KEEP AN EYE ON THEM."

"THE PACOHS WERE SHOCKED AND AMAZED. LEAVE PARADISE TO BECOME STARVING REFUGEES IN THE BACK STREET SEWERS, WORKING FOR SLAVE WAGES ON THE FILTHY DOCKS LIKE FISH OUT OF WATER?"

"WHY?"

"SEVERAL ORDERS WERE SENT. THE PACOHS IGNORED THEM. THE SIAGON GOVERNMENT TOOK IT AS A SLAP IN THE FACE. HEAVY HANDEDNESS DID NOT WORK, THEY WOULD EMPLOY TREACHERY."

"THE GOVERNMENT CALLED ALL OF THE VILLAGE CHIEFS TO HUE FOR WHAT THEY SAID WERE JUST MEETINGS TO DISCUSS THE PROBLEM. THEY WERE UNCEREMONIOUSLY THROWN IN PRISON AND WORD WAS SENT BACK THAT THEY WOULD REMAIN IN PRISON UNTIL THE TRIBES CAPITULATED."

"THE SIMPLE TRIBES PEOPLE WERE CONFUSED AND COMPLETELY HORRIFIED BY THE ACT OF DECEIT. THEY HAD NO FRAME OF REFERENCE."

"THEY GRIEVED FOR THEIR CHIEFS BUT THEY DID NOT COME DOWN."

"PRESIDENT DIEM WAS FURIOUS! HE ORDERED HEAVILY ARMED TROOPS INTO THE ASHAU TO ROUND UP THE VILLAGERS, BUT THEY SIMPLY DISAPPEARED INTO THE JUNGLE."

"THE PACOHS WATCHED FROM THEIR HIDING PLACES AS THE TROOPS BURNED THEIR HOMES AND DESTROYED THEIR CROPS. THEIR ENTIRE LIVES WENT UP IN FLAMES."

"AFTER DESTROYING EVERYTHING IN THEIR PATH THE ARVN SOLDIERS WITHDREW AND THE SIMPLE TRIBESFOLK BEGAN TO REBUILD..."

"NOT TO BE OUTDONE, THE VIET CONG, AFRAID OF LOSING THE PACOHS TO THE SIAGON GOVERNMENT, COLLECTED EVERY ABLE BODIED MAN AND FORCE MARCHED THEM OFF TO LAOS AS SLAVES TO WORK ON THE HO CHI MINH TRAIL."

"WHEN THE TRIBAL CHIEF REFUSED TO GO HE WAS BEHEADED AND HIS DAUGHTER VIOLATED IN FRONT OF THE WHOLE VILLAGE!"

"HE SAYS IT WAS THAT MOMENT WHEN HE DECIDED THAT THERE WOULD COME A DAY WHEN HE WOULD MAKE BOTH THE ARVN AND VIET CONG PAY."

"THE PACOHS WERE SCATTERED TO THE FOUR WINDS, ONLY A HANDFUL WERE ABLE TO ESCAPE ABUSE FROM BOTH ARMIES. OVER 40 VILLAGES WITH SEVERAL THOUSAND OF HIS NATIVE FELLOWS WERE DESTROYED."

"HE SPENT HIS TEEN YEARS UNDER THE THUMB OF THE VIET CONG, FORCED TO LABOR IN ALL KINDS OF WEATHER, ON LITTLE SLEEP AND ON AS LITTLE AS A HANDFUL OF RICE A DAY."

"THE NUMBER OF PACOHS DWINDLED STILL FURTHER WITH MANY DYING FROM INSECT AND SNAKE BITES, OTHERS FROM MALARIA, AND STILL OTHERS MURDERED AT THEIR VIET CONG CAPTOR'S WHIM!"

"LIFE WAS CHEAP ON THE HO CHI MINH TRAIL, AND A PACOH LIFE WAS CHEAPER STILL!"

"THE TIME PRESSURES FOR THE VIET CONG WERE INTENSE. HANOI HAD EARLIER COMMITTED TO THE FLOOD INTO THE SOUTH WITH THOUSANDS OF NORTH VIETNAMESE TROOPS AND EQUIPMENT TO SUPPORT THEM."

"THE BULK OF WHICH WOULD BE DELIVERED OVER THE HO CHI MINH TRAIL."

"THE A SHAU VALLEY WAS A NATURAL FOR THE NORTH VIETNAMESE TO DEVELOP AS AN EXTENSIVE STAGING AREA AND WEAPONS DEPOT. NVA TROOPS FLOODED SOUTH."

"AND, OF COURSE, BY 1964, ARVN TROOPS IN CONJUNCTION WITH UNITED STATES SPECIAL FORCES UNITS BEGAN ESTABLISHING FOOT-HOLDS IN THE A SHAU TO COUNTERACT THE ENEMY THREAT."

"HE SUFFERED IN SILENCE, HARDLY NOTICED BY THE NVA CADRE, UNTIL SIMPLY BY ATTRITION, HE ROSE TO BE A SENIOR MEMBER OF HIS PARTICULAR WORK DETAIL."

"FINALLY HE WAS RECOGNIZED FOR HIS YEARS OF HARD WORK AND SENT TO HANOI TO BE INDOCTRINATED INTO THE COMMUNIST MINDSET."

"WHEN HE RETURNED HE WAS A CARD CARRYING MEMBER OF THE COMMUNIST PARTY... A TOKEN MONTAGNARD FOR DISPLAY."

"BECAUSE OF HIS EXTENSIVE KNOWLEDGE OF THE A SHAU HE WAS GIVEN A MEASURE OF FREEDOM TO PATROL THE A SHAU WITH SQUADS OF VIET CONG TO LOG AMERICAN AND ARVN MOVEMENTS."

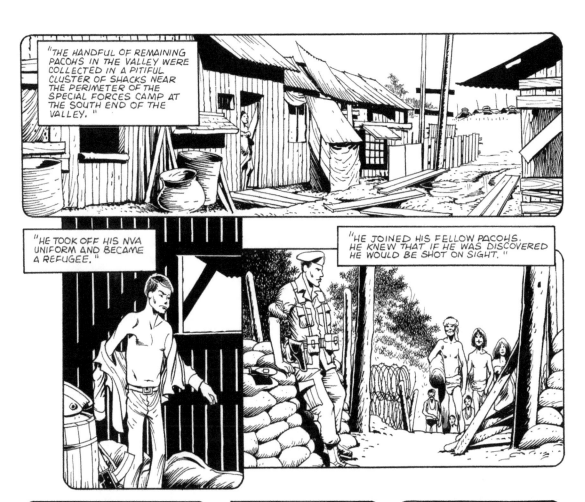

"THE HANDFUL OF REMAINING PACOHS IN THE VALLEY WERE COLLECTED IN A PITIFUL CLUSTER OF SHACKS NEAR THE PERIMETER OF THE SPECIAL FORCES CAMP AT THE SOUTH END OF THE VALLEY."

"HE TOOK OFF HIS NVA UNIFORM AND BECAME A REFUGEE."

"HE JOINED HIS FELLOW PACOHS. HE KNEW THAT IF HE WAS DISCOVERED HE WOULD BE SHOT ON SIGHT."

"HE ARRANGED WITH THE SURVIVING ELDER TO PASS INFORMATION ABOUT NVA TROOP MOVEMENTS TO THE AMERICANS. WITH THAT HE BECAME A VALUABLE COMMODITY, THOUGH THE AMERICANS WERE HESITANT TO USE THE INFORMATION."

"BUT AS THE MONTHS WENT BY, AND MORE AND MORE OF HIS INFORMATION PROVED OUT..."

"...THE MORE NORTH VIETNAMESE TROOPS FELL TO AMERICAN BOMBING AND AIR STRIKES."

"HE FELT NO ALLEGIANCE TO THE NORTH VIETNAMESE. THOUGH HE WORE THEIR UNIFORM AND ATE THEIR RICE HE HAD NO MORE REGARD FOR THEM THAN HE DID FOR THE SOUTH VIETNAMESE."

"AND WHEN THEY DIED BY THE HUNDREDS HE FELT ONLY SATISFACTION."

"BOTH SIDES WERE TREACHEROUS DOGS IN HIS EYES AND HE COULD NEVER FORGIVE THEM FOR BRINGING WAR TO HIS VALLEY."

"HE HATED THE BLACK RIFLES LEAST ONLY BECAUSE HE HATED THE NORTH AND SOUTH VIET-NAMESE SO VERY MUCH!"

"HE FOUND THAT NOT ONLY COULD HE PASS INFORMATION TO THE SOUTH VIETNAMESE ABOUT NVA TROOP MOVEMENTS AND WEAPONS CASHES. HE INTURN WAS ABLE TO FIND OUT VOLUMES ABOUT SOUTH VIETNAMESE TROOPS AND THEIR MOVEMENTS AND LOCATIONS."

"BEFORE LONG HE BECAME A DOUBLE AGENT IN THE TRUEST SENSE OF THE WORD. BOTH SIDES UNDER-ESTIMATING HIS RESOLVE."

"HIS DISGUST FOR HIS OWN PEOPLE GREW, THEY LIVED OFF DISCARDS AND GARBAGE FROM THE KITCHENS OF THE SPECIAL FORCES CAMP. THE WAR HAD BROKEN THEM. IT WOULD NOT BREAK HIM."

"THEN THE NEWS CAME OF AN IMPENDING ATTACK OF THE SPECIAL FORCES CAMP. ARMED WITH THE INFORMATION HE CHOSE TO SURRENDER TO WARN THE AMERICANS."

"HE WAS UP FRONT WITH HIS REASONS FOR WARNING THEM BUT STILL THE ARVN INTERROGATED HIM SEVERELY FOR SEVERAL DAYS..."

"BEFORE THE CAMP FELL HE WAS EVACUATED TO BE REPATRIOTED."

"...UNTIL THEIR ATTENTION WAS DRAWN ELSEWHERE BY ENEMY PROBING AND INTELLIGENCE OF A MAJOR ENEMY BUILD-UP."

"IT WAS THE OFFICIALS DETERMINATION THAT HE WAS AN IDEAL CANDIDATE FOR THE CHIEU HOI AMNESTY PROGRAM."

VINH LONG

CHIEU HOI

"WHILE HE WAS BEING INDOCTRINATED THE AMERICANS AND ARYN TROOPS RETREATED ON THEIR WILD EXODUS FROM THE A SHAU..."

"...NOT TO RETURN..."

"...FOR A FULL THREE YEARS!"

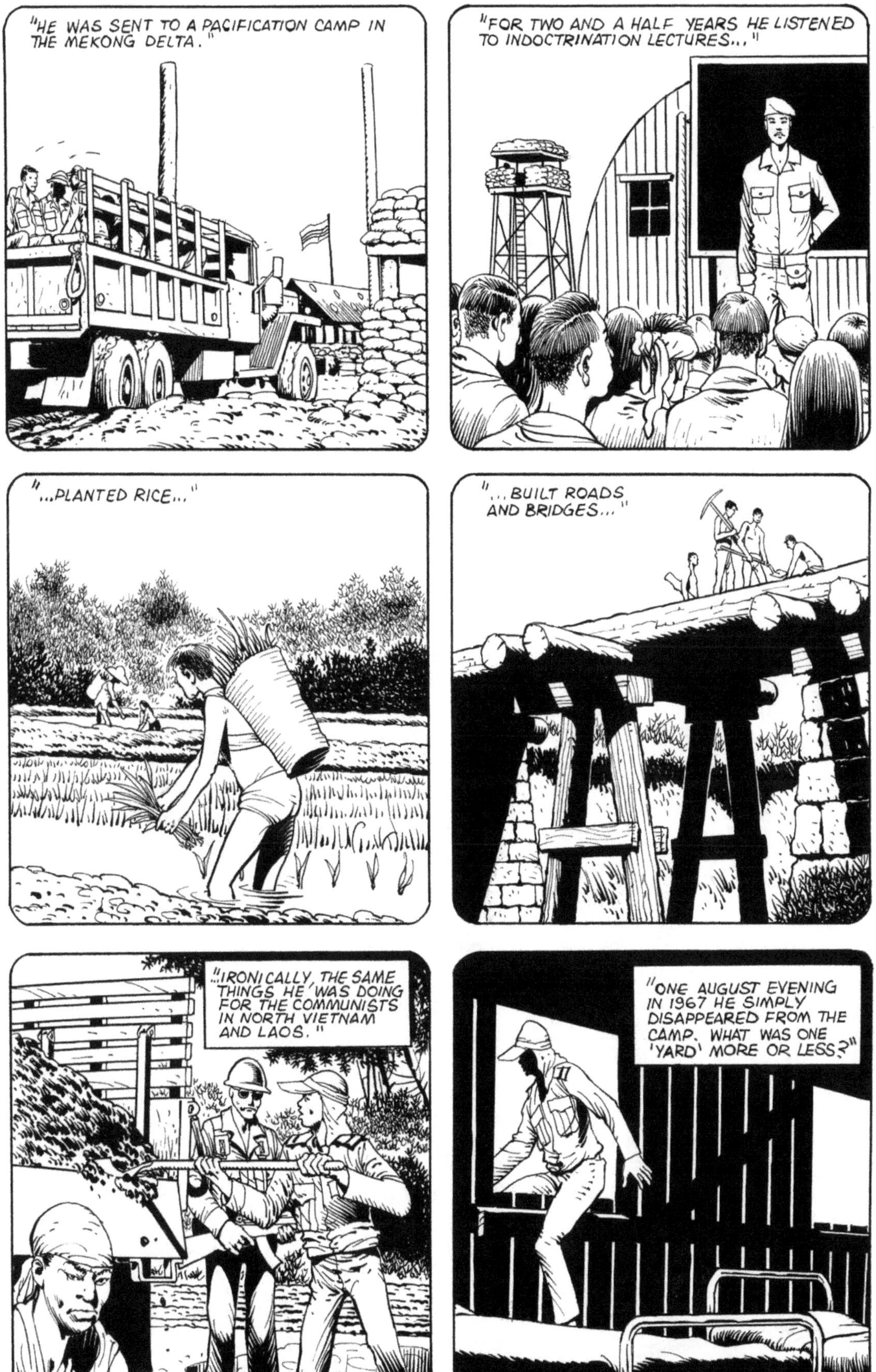
"HE WAS SENT TO A PACIFICATION CAMP IN THE MEKONG DELTA."
"FOR TWO AND A HALF YEARS HE LISTENED TO INDOCTRINATION LECTURES..."
"...PLANTED RICE..."
"...BUILT ROADS AND BRIDGES..."
"...IRONICALLY, THE SAME THINGS HE WAS DOING FOR THE COMMUNISTS IN NORTH VIETNAM AND LAOS."
"ONE AUGUST EVENING IN 1967 HE SIMPLY DISAPPEARED FROM THE CAMP. WHAT WAS ONE 'YARD' MORE OR LESS?"

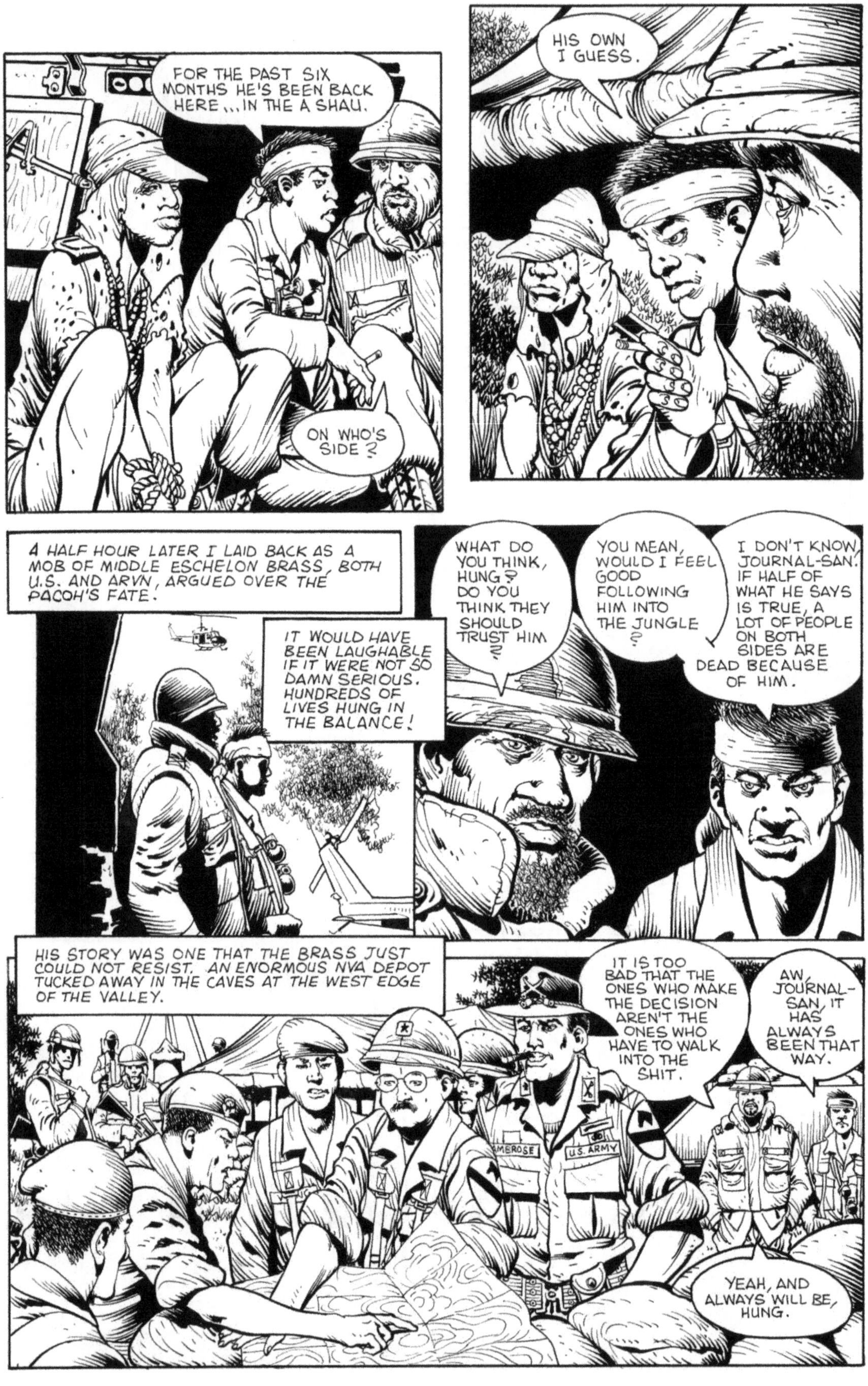

FOR THE PAST SIX MONTHS HE'S BEEN BACK HERE ... IN THE A SHAU.
ON WHO'S SIDE?
HIS OWN I GUESS.
A HALF HOUR LATER I LAID BACK AS A MOB OF MIDDLE ESCHELON BRASS, BOTH U.S. AND ARVN, ARGUED OVER THE PACOH'S FATE.
IT WOULD HAVE BEEN LAUGHABLE IF IT WERE NOT SO DAMN SERIOUS. HUNDREDS OF LIVES HUNG IN THE BALANCE!
WHAT DO YOU THINK, HUNG? DO YOU THINK THEY SHOULD TRUST HIM?
YOU MEAN, WOULD I FEEL GOOD FOLLOWING HIM INTO THE JUNGLE?
I DON'T KNOW, JOURNAL-SAN. IF HALF OF WHAT HE SAYS IS TRUE, A LOT OF PEOPLE ON BOTH SIDES ARE DEAD BECAUSE OF HIM.
HIS STORY WAS ONE THAT THE BRASS JUST COULD NOT RESIST. AN ENORMOUS NVA DEPOT TUCKED AWAY IN THE CAVES AT THE WEST EDGE OF THE VALLEY.
U.S. ARMY
IT IS TOO BAD THAT THE ONES WHO MAKE THE DECISION AREN'T THE ONES WHO HAVE TO WALK INTO THE SHIT.
AW, JOURNAL-SAN, IT HAS ALWAYS BEEN THAT WAY.
YEAH, AND ALWAYS WILL BE, HUNG.

I HAD A BAD FEELING ABOUT THIS OPERATION. EVEN THOUGH WE MOVED OUT AT COMPANY STRENGTH WITH SUFFICIENT FIREPOWER TO HANDLE ALMOST ANY SITUATION AND WITH ARTILLERY AND AIR SUPPORT AT OUR BECKON CALL, IF WE NEEDED IT.

WE NEEDED IT.

THA-BOOM

THE ENTIRE JUNGLE LIT UP!

I KNEW IT... GOD DAMN IT! I KNEW IT!

WELL, THE PACOH KNEW HOW TO FIND THE NORTH VIETNAMESE IF THAT WAS WHAT COMMAND WANTED.

BUT AS I SQUIRMED ACROSS TREMBLING GROUND DESPERATE FOR COVER, I WONDERED IF WE FOUND THEM OR THEY FOUND US.

HUNG SQUEALED AND WENT DOWN, A PIECE OF HIS KNEE MISSING!

I PULLED HUNG TO COVER AND GLANCED AROUND

WHERE IS HE? WHERE'S THE PACOH?

SKYRAIDERS CAME IN LOW OVER THE TREETOPS...

...NAPALM CANISTERS TUMBLED DOWN, END OVER END, LIKE SLOW MOTION.

HEAT ROLLED OVER US LIKE AN OCEAN WAVE!

I TURNED MY ATTENTION TO HUNG. THE BULLET HAD CLIPPED THE MAIN ARTERY IN HIS LEG. HIS FACE WAS ASHEN. I WAS AFRAID HE WAS GOING INTO SHOCK.

JUST STAYING ALIVE AND CONTROLLING HUNG'S BLEEDING OCCUPIED ME FOR WHAT SEEMED A LIFETIME.

A FLURRY OF ROCKETS FELL ON OUR POSITION...

...RECOILLESS RIFLE AND MACHINE GUN FIRE FROM THE HILLS TO OUR FRONT PINNED US DOWN.

THEN THE SKY RAIDERS WERE BACK...

...TO FRY THE ENEMY SOLDIERS...

...FOLLOWED BY SECONDARY EXPLOSIONS ROCKING THE GROUND UNDER US!

THE JUNGLE ERUPTED IN A SERIES OF EXPLOSIONS AS THE NVA MAGAZINES WENT UP!

BURN, BABY, BURN!

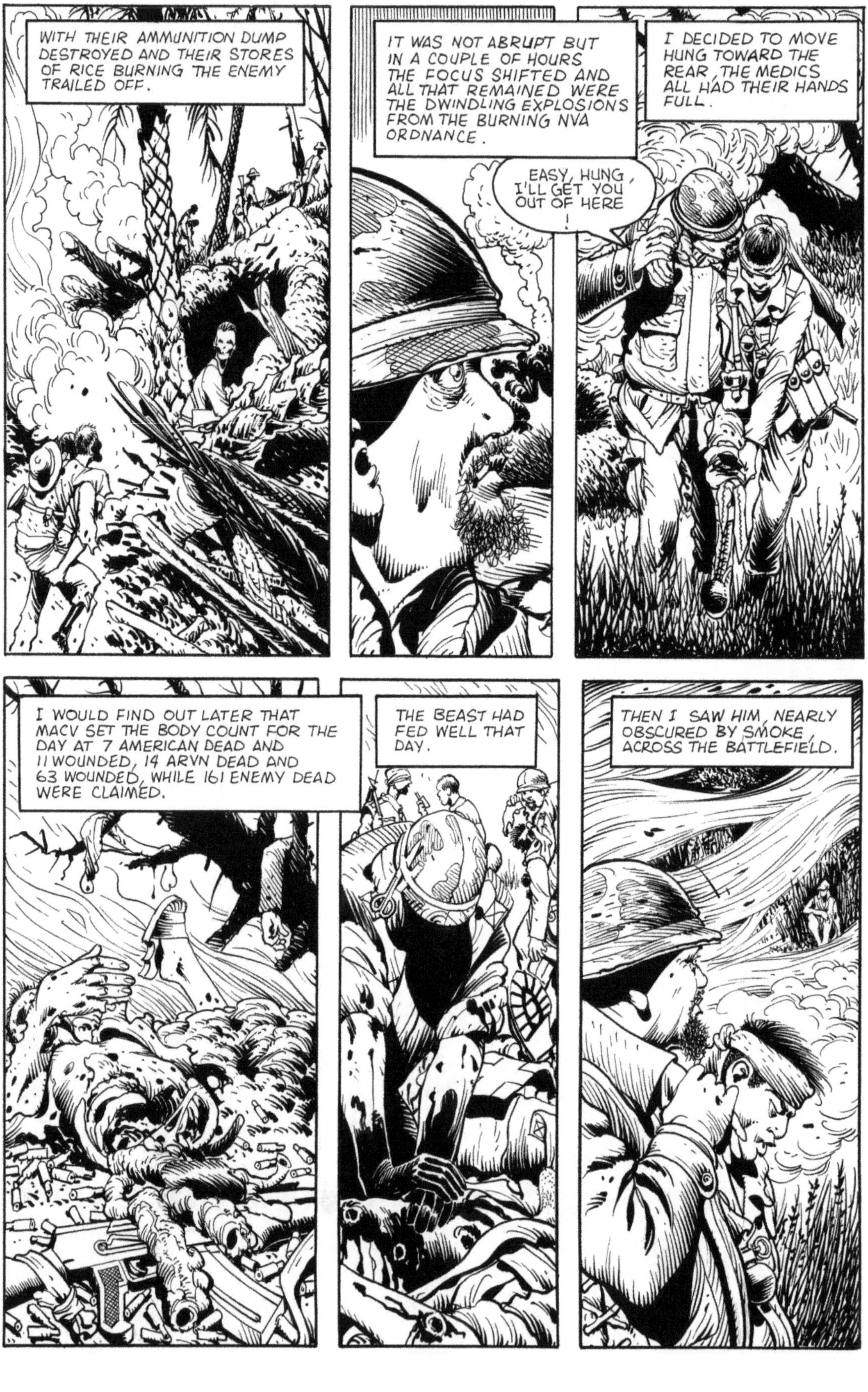
WITH THEIR AMMUNITION DUMP DESTROYED AND THEIR STORES OF RICE BURNING THE ENEMY TRAILED OFF.
IT WAS NOT ABRUPT BUT IN A COUPLE OF HOURS THE FOCUS SHIFTED AND ALL THAT REMAINED WERE THE DWINDLING EXPLOSIONS FROM THE BURNING NVA ORDNANCE.
EASY, HUNG, I'LL GET YOU OUT OF HERE!
I DECIDED TO MOVE HUNG TOWARD THE REAR, THE MEDICS ALL HAD THEIR HANDS FULL.
I WOULD FIND OUT LATER THAT MACV SET THE BODY COUNT FOR THE DAY AT 7 AMERICAN DEAD AND 11 WOUNDED, 14 ARVN DEAD AND 63 WOUNDED, WHILE 161 ENEMY DEAD WERE CLAIMED.
THE BEAST HAD FED WELL THAT DAY.
THEN I SAW HIM, NEARLY OBSCURED BY SMOKE, ACROSS THE BATTLEFIELD.

OR DID I !?

HE SEEMED TO FADE AWAY. I AM NOT SURE TO THIS DAY IF I REALLY SAW HIM.

MACV TERMED THE OPERATION A SUCCESS, THOUGH THERE WAS PLENTY OF DEAD ON BOTH SIDES.

FIELD TRIAGE IS THIS WAY, JOURNAL. DUST OFF IN TEN MIKES.

I GUESS THE ONLY WINNER WAS THE PACOH.

YEAH, WELL, MAYBE IT WAS HIS TURN.

MOVE IT GRANDPA!

NEXT: REGROUP

Missing American

C-130 and it's entire crew lost and MIA in Laos

The following profiles nine of those Missing Americans:

Just following the Marine Corps operation Pegasus/Lam Son 207 in mid-April 1968, to relieve the siege of Khe Sanh, Operation Scotland II began in the Khe Sanh area, more or less as a continuation of this support effort. The C130 was critical in resupplying this area, and when the C130 could not land, it dropped its payload by means of parachute drop.

One of the bases from which the C130 flew was Ubon, located in northeast Thailand. C130 crews from this base crossed Laos to their objective location. One such crew was comprised of:

LtCol. William H. Mason, *Pilot*
Capt. Thomas B. Mitchell, *Pilot*
Capt. William T McPhail, *crew*
Maj. Jerry L. Chambers, *crew*
SA Gary Pate, *crew*
SSgt. Calvin C, Glover, *crew*
AM1 Melvin D. Rash, *crew*
AM1 John Quincy Adams, *crew*
AM1 Thomas E. Knebel, *passenger*

On May 22, 1968, this crew departed Ubon on an operational mission in a C130A carrying one passenger—Knebel. Radio contact was lost while the aircraft was over Savannakhet Province, Laos near the city of Muong Nong, (suggesting that its target area may have been near the DMZ—Khe Sanh). When the aircraft did not return to friendly control, the crew was declared Missing In Action from the time of estimated fuel exhaustion. There was no further word of the aircraft on its crew.

Since the end of the Vietnam War there have been more than 21,000 reports received by our government about American prisoners, missing, and otherwise unaccounted for personnel. Many of these reports were from actual eye witnesses in the Southeast Asian theater and document LIVE Americans being held captive even today. How long will we allow this tragedy to continue?

American servicemen served selflessly and in harm's way in the decade long struggle in Southeast Asia to include Vietnam, Laos, Cambodia, and Thailand, were wounded, taken prisoner, and killed as witnessed by the 58,000 name on the black slab wall of remembrance in Washington D.C. Every missing fighting man who served in the Vietnam War deserves to be accounted for. America has always taken pride in leaving no fighting man behind. What can yo do? Educate yourself on this subject.

Vietnam Journal
Valley of
DEATH

REGROUP

REGROUP

NO MORE WAR

STOP THE WAR

HELL NO WE WON'T GO!

LINCOLN PAR[K]

CHICAGO POLICE

Vietnam Journal™
Valley of
DEATH™

THE SUMMER AND FALL OF 1968 WERE AN ENDLESS BLUR OF WAR, CONFUSION, PAIN, AND SUFFERING AS THE "BEAST" FED RELENTLESS. IN LATE AUGUST ANTIWAR PROTESTS AND RIOTS AT THE DEMOCRATIC CONVENTION IN CHICAGO ECHOED AMERICA'S FRUSTRATION WITH THE VIETNAM WAR.

SO FRUSTRATED, THAT RICHARD NIXON'S "SECRET PLAN" TO END THE WAR WAS BOUGHT HOOK-LINE-AND-SINKER BY A DESPERATE POPULATION ALLOWING NIXON TO DEFEAT HUBERT HUMPHREY IN THE ELECTION FOR PRESIDENT OF THE UNITED STATES ON NOVEMBER 5, 1968.

STORY AND ART
DON LOMAX

I WAS IN AND OUT OF THE A SHAU REPEATEDLY OVER THE NEXT SEVERAL MONTHS. I CONTINUED MY REPORTING AROUND SOUTH VIETNAM BUT MY PRIMARY INTEREST REMAINED THE A SHAU.

AS 1969 BEGAN AND RICHARD NIXON REPLACED LYNDON JOHNSON AS PRESIDENT, I WAS SPENDING FAR TOO MUCH TIME WITH A BEER IN MY HAND.
OLD HABITS DIE HARD.

OPERATIONS CAME AND WENT BUT STILL THE A SHAU HAUNTED ME. I CONTINUED LOGGING MY STORIES, MANY OF WHICH I SHALL CHRONICLE IN THESE PAGES AT A FUTURE DATE, BUT THE A SHAU KEPT RETURNING LIKE BAD CHILI FROM RUSS'S TIRE AND GAS CAFE AND TRUCKWASH.

I HAD WITNESSED DEBAUCHERY BEFORE BUT THE "BOOM-BOOM ROOMS" OF DISNEY-LAND EAST IN THE CENTRAL HIGHLANDS AT AN KHE WERE BEGINNING TO BE MY HOME AWAY FROM HOME.

WITH LITTLE LAW AND ORDER THE BROTHELS, BARS, AND BATH HOUSES THRIVED TO SERVICE THE FIRST AIR CAVALRY BACK WHEN AN KHE WAS HOME FOR THE "BLANKET BRIGADE".

BY '69 THE BOOM HAD GONE BUST AND THE SHANTY TOWN WAS A HOLLOW, MUDDLED, VIOLENT PLACE. IN SOME WAYS MORE DANGEROUS THAN THE BUSH!

THE WAR WAS AN ALL-ENCOMPASSING BLIGHT. IT INEVITABLY SPILLED OVER INTO THE TROOPERS OFF-HOURS. IT COULD NOT BE TURNED OFF LIKE A FAUCET.

GRENADE!!

JESUS H. CHRIST!

MY NAME'S SCOTT NEITHAMMER, THE TROOPS CALL ME JOURNAL.

BUSTED.

HEY, JOURNAL... WHERE YA GOIN', MAN? THE PARTY'S JUST STARTED!

I'M HEADED BACK TO THE A-SHAU... IT'S TOO DANGEROUS HERE.

OVER THE PAST YEAR THERE HAD BEEN A LOT OF GIVE AND TAKE FROM BOTH SIDES IN THE A SHAU.

MILITARY ASSISTANCE COMMAND VIETNAM (MACV) HAD COMMITTED AN INTENSE EFFORT TO CLEAR THE A SHAU OF NORTH VIETNAMESE, AND THOUGH INROADS WERE MADE STILL THE ENEMY HELD ON STUBBORNLY.

I WAS BEGINNING TO NEED IT. LIKE OTHER FRONTLINE GRUNTS WHO WERE LIKE FISH OUT OF WATER IN THE REAR. MORE THAN A MONTH WITHOUT BEING SHOT AT WAS A MONTH WASTED.

THOUGH I WOULD NEVER HAVE ADMITTED IT AT THE TIME, I WAS BECOMING A FULL BLOWN ADRENALINE JUNKY!

AS I CAUGHT A RIDE BACK INTO THE VALLEY IT WAS STRANGELY MORE FOR MY OWN SANITY THAN FOR DUTY. I TRIED NOT TO THINK ABOUT WHAT I WAS BECOMING.

THE JUNGLE BELOW US WAS LUSH AS WE SKIMMED THE TREETOPS TO FACE WHAT THE 101ST AIRBORNE TROOPS WOULD SOON BE REFERRING TO AS "BLOODY RIDGE". IT WOULD EARN ITS NAME HONESTLY.

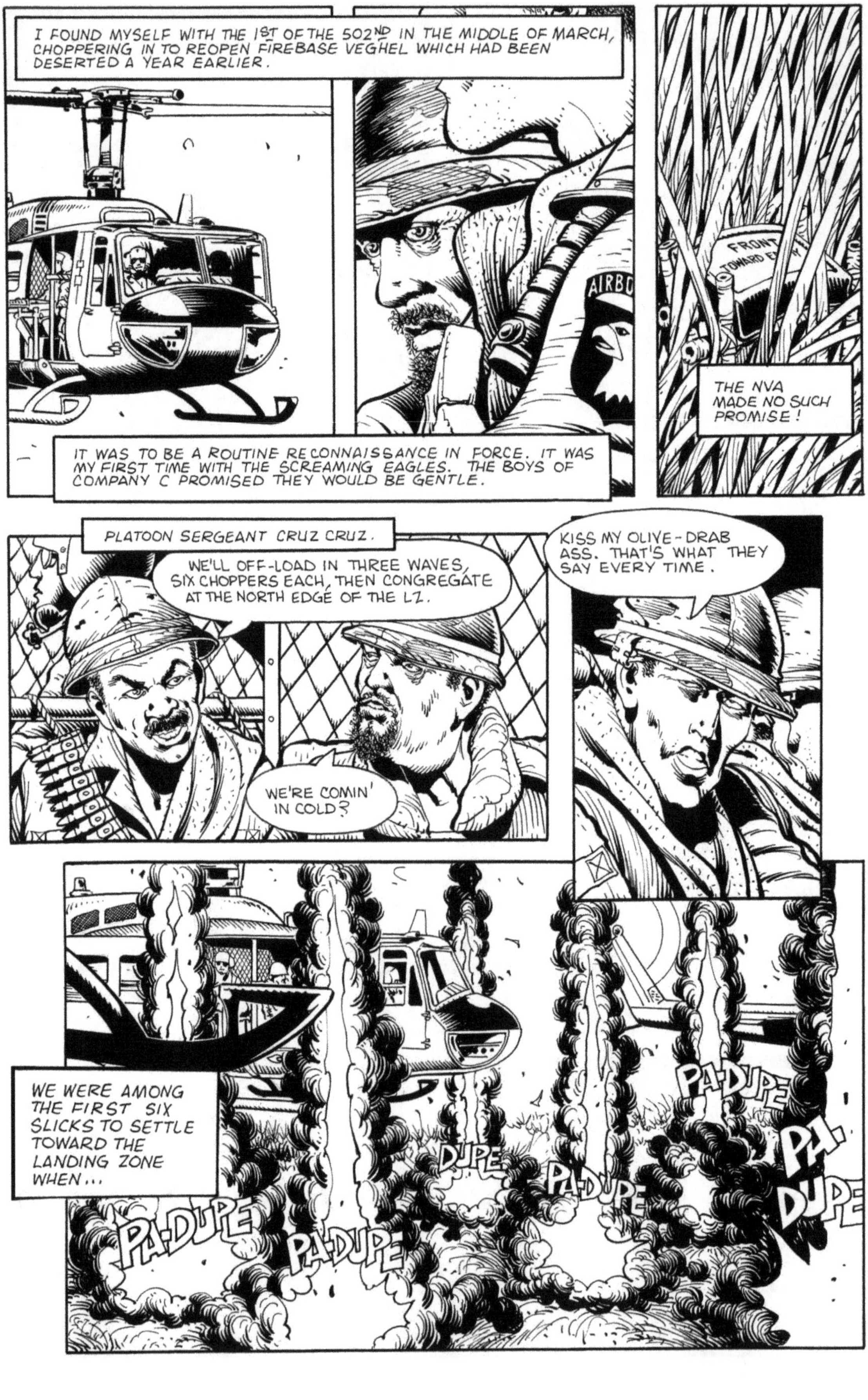

I FOUND MYSELF WITH THE 1ST OF THE 502ND IN THE MIDDLE OF MARCH, CHOPPERING IN TO REOPEN FIREBASE VEGHEL WHICH HAD BEEN DESERTED A YEAR EARLIER.
IT WAS TO BE A ROUTINE RECONNAISSANCE IN FORCE. IT WAS MY FIRST TIME WITH THE SCREAMING EAGLES. THE BOYS OF COMPANY C PROMISED THEY WOULD BE GENTLE.
THE NVA MADE NO SUCH PROMISE!
PLATOON SERGEANT CRUZ CRUZ.
WE'LL OFF-LOAD IN THREE WAVES, SIX CHOPPERS EACH, THEN CONGREGATE AT THE NORTH EDGE OF THE LZ.
WE'RE COMIN' IN COLD?
KISS MY OLIVE-DRAB ASS. THAT'S WHAT THEY SAY EVERY TIME.
WE WERE AMONG THE FIRST SIX SLICKS TO SETTLE TOWARD THE LANDING ZONE WHEN...
PA-DUPE
PA-DUPE
DUPE
PA-DUPE
PA-DUPE
PA-DUPE

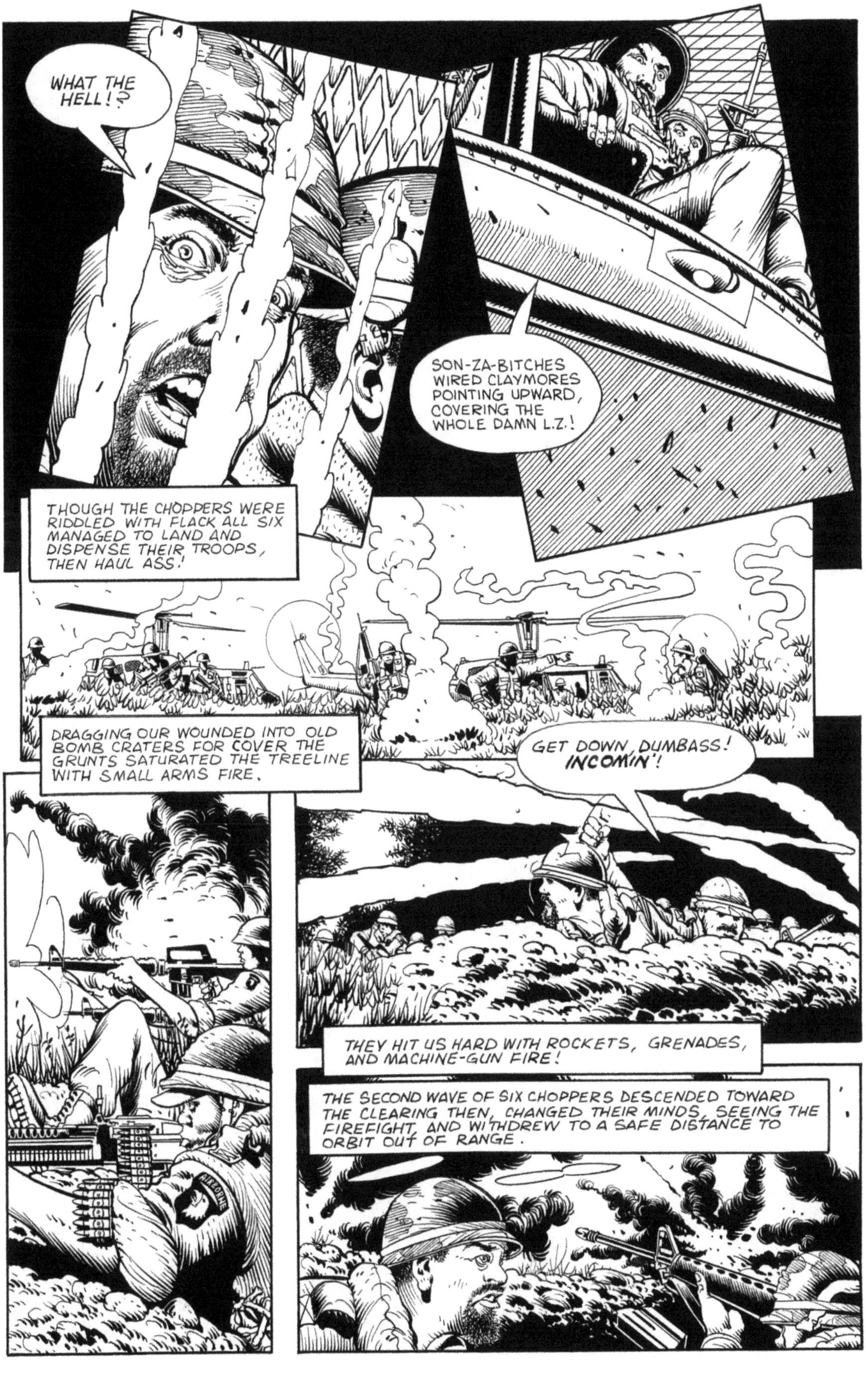
WHAT THE HELL!?
SON-ZA-BITCHES WIRED CLAYMORES POINTING UPWARD, COVERING THE WHOLE DAMN L.Z.!
THOUGH THE CHOPPERS WERE RIDDLED WITH FLACK ALL SIX MANAGED TO LAND AND DISPENSE THEIR TROOPS, THEN HAUL ASS!
DRAGGING OUR WOUNDED INTO OLD BOMB CRATERS FOR COVER THE GRUNTS SATURATED THE TREELINE WITH SMALL ARMS FIRE.
GET DOWN, DUMBASS! INCOMIN'!
THEY HIT US HARD WITH ROCKETS, GRENADES, AND MACHINE-GUN FIRE!
THE SECOND WAVE OF SIX CHOPPERS DESCENDED TOWARD THE CLEARING THEN, CHANGED THEIR MINDS, SEEING THE FIREFIGHT, AND WITHDREW TO A SAFE DISTANCE TO ORBIT OUT OF RANGE.

THEY'RE CHARGING! EVERYBODY ON THE LINE!

THE NVA CHARGED US TWICE BUT WERE DRIVEN BACK BOTH TIMES.

SERGEANT BLAKE, SIT-REP!

OVER HALF OF THE PLATOON IS WOUNDED, SARGE. WE AIN'T GONNA WITHSTAND ANOTHER ATTACK.

HAVE THE RTO GET BUCKET-BUTT ON THE HORN. WE NEED NAPALM ON THAT TREELINE AND WE NEED IT ASAP.

AND THE HEAT FROM THE AIR STRIKE ONLY A FEW METERS AWAY ROLLED OVER US TO SINGE THE BACK OF MY NECK.

THA-BOOOOM

AS THE ENEMY MASSED FOR THEIR THIRD ATTACK ON OUR TENUOUS POSITION THE F-4'S APPEARED AS IF BY MAGIC.

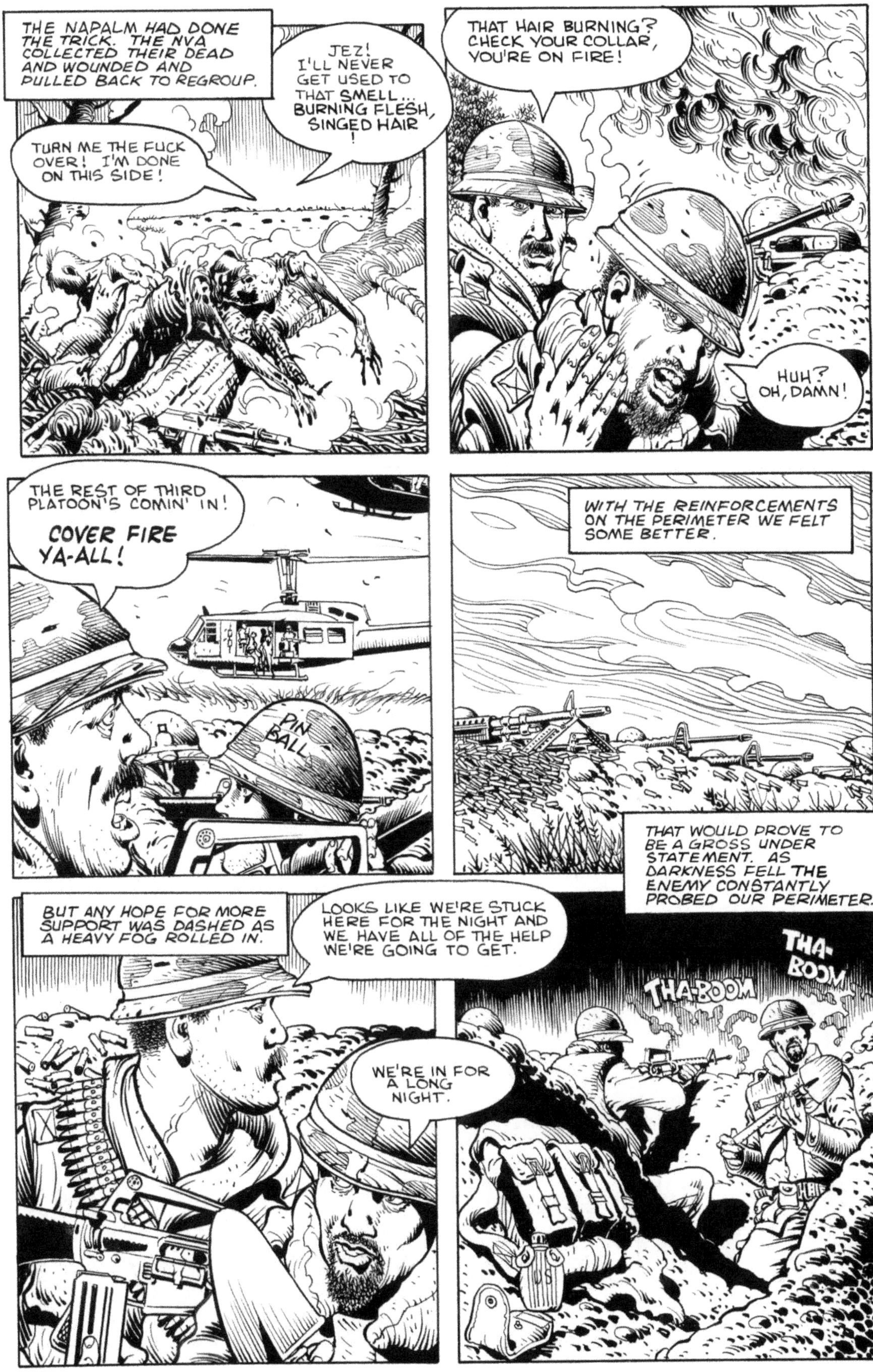
THE NAPALM HAD DONE THE TRICK. THE NVA COLLECTED THEIR DEAD AND WOUNDED AND PULLED BACK TO REGROUP.
JEZ! I'LL NEVER GET USED TO THAT SMELL... BURNING FLESH, SINGED HAIR!
TURN ME THE FUCK OVER! I'M DONE ON THIS SIDE!
THAT HAIR BURNING? CHECK YOUR COLLAR, YOU'RE ON FIRE!
HUH? OH, DAMN!
THE REST OF THIRD PLATOON'S COMIN' IN!
COVER FIRE YA-ALL!
PIN BALL
WITH THE REINFORCEMENTS ON THE PERIMETER WE FELT SOME BETTER.
BUT ANY HOPE FOR MORE SUPPORT WAS DASHED AS A HEAVY FOG ROLLED IN.
LOOKS LIKE WE'RE STUCK HERE FOR THE NIGHT AND WE HAVE ALL OF THE HELP WE'RE GOING TO GET.
WE'RE IN FOR A LONG NIGHT.
THAT WOULD PROVE TO BE A GROSS UNDER STATEMENT. AS DARKNESS FELL THE ENEMY CONSTANTLY PROBED OUR PERIMETER.
THA-BOOM
THA-BOOM

NO ONE SLEPT. THE FLURRY OF GUNFIRE CONTINUALLY ERUPTED UP AND DOWN THE LINE AS THE WEATHER YOYOED FROM FOG TO RAIN AND BACK TO FOG REPEATEDLY.

OUR ONLY RELIEF WAS DURING THE BRIEF PERIODS WHEN THE DOWNPOUR DROWNED OUT THE SOUNDS OF BATTLE.

BUT THOSE TIMES WERE THE MOST DANGEROUS. NVA TROOPS COULD SNEAK RIGHT UP ON US IN THE RAIN UNTIL...

JOURNAL! WAKE THE FUCK UP!

SMAT

GET RID OF IT! FOR CHRIST'S SAKE, GET RID OF IT!

FFFISSSSS

FISSSSSSSSSS

GASP!

THUMP

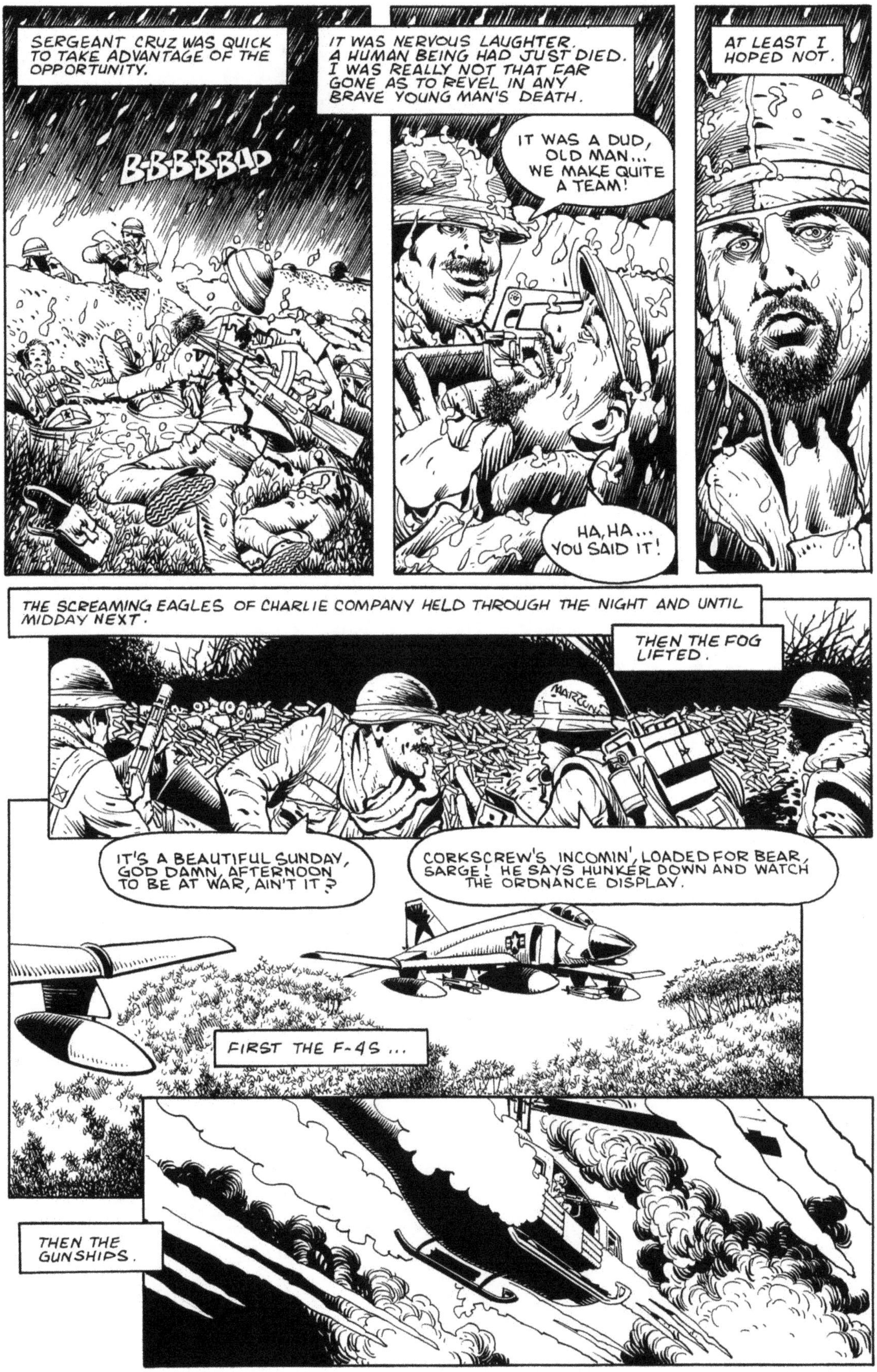
SERGEANT CRUZ WAS QUICK TO TAKE ADVANTAGE OF THE OPPORTUNITY.
B-B-B-B-BAP
IT WAS NERVOUS LAUGHTER. A HUMAN BEING HAD JUST DIED. I WAS REALLY NOT THAT FAR GONE AS TO REVEL IN ANY BRAVE YOUNG MAN'S DEATH.
IT WAS A DUD, OLD MAN... WE MAKE QUITE A TEAM!
HA, HA... YOU SAID IT!
AT LEAST I HOPED NOT.
THE SCREAMING EAGLES OF CHARLIE COMPANY HELD THROUGH THE NIGHT AND UNTIL MIDDAY NEXT.
THEN THE FOG LIFTED.
IT'S A BEAUTIFUL SUNDAY, GOD DAMN, AFTERNOON TO BE AT WAR, AIN'T IT?
CORKSCREW'S INCOMIN', LOADED FOR BEAR, SARGE! HE SAYS HUNKER DOWN AND WATCH THE ORDNANCE DISPLAY.
FIRST THE F-4S ...
THEN THE GUNSHIPS.

TAKING ADVANTAGE OF THE DIVERSION, THE REST OF THE BATTALION WAS AIR LIFTED INTO THE A.O..

WITH A REINFORCED BATTALION TO DEAL WITH AND THE AIRSTRIKES HAMMERING THEM INTO THE GROUND, THE NORTH VIETNAMESE HAD ENOUGH, ABANDONED THEIR DEFENSES AND TRIED TO ESCAPE DEEPER INTO THE A SHAU.

FOR THIRTY-THREE DAYS THE SCREAMING EAGLES WAGED A RUNNING GUNBATTLE THAT RIVALLED ANY ACTION I HAD EVER WITNESSED.

YOU OKAY, JOURNAL?

I'M TOO OLD FOR THIS... HOW CAN I BE HOT AND COLD AT THE SAME TIME?

BUCKET-BUTT SAYS THAT THE NORTH VIETNAMESE ARE GONNA MAKE A STAND ON THAT HILL. THEY THINK HIS BACK'S AGAINST THE WALL. THEY EXPECT AN EXTENSIVE COMPLEX ALONG THAT RIDGE. LOOKS LIKE THIS IS IT. IT'S GONNA BE MESSY.

THESE WERE HARDCORE REGULARS. THERE WAS EVERY EVIDENCE THAT THEY WERE PREPARED TO FIGHT TO THE LAST MAN. THAT WAS OKAY WITH THE SCREAMING EAGLES. AFTER A MONTH OF DISAPPOINT- MENT THE 101ST HAD A GIANT CASE OF BLUEBALLS.

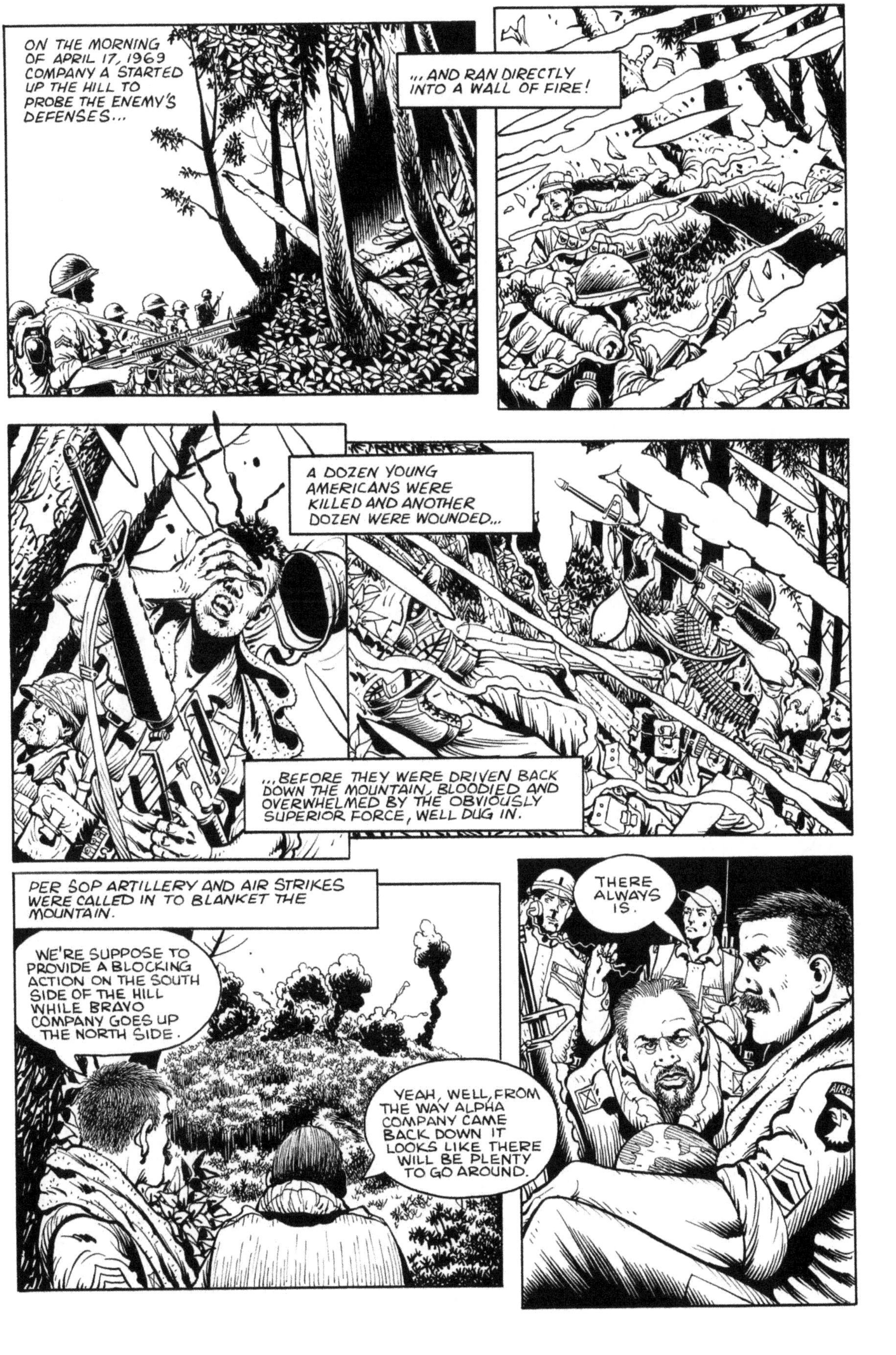
ON THE MORNING OF APRIL 17, 1969 COMPANY A STARTED UP THE HILL TO PROBE THE ENEMY'S DEFENSES...
...AND RAN DIRECTLY INTO A WALL OF FIRE!
A DOZEN YOUNG AMERICANS WERE KILLED AND ANOTHER DOZEN WERE WOUNDED...
...BEFORE THEY WERE DRIVEN BACK DOWN THE MOUNTAIN, BLOODIED AND OVERWHELMED BY THE OBVIOUSLY SUPERIOR FORCE, WELL DUG IN.
PER SOP ARTILLERY AND AIR STRIKES WERE CALLED IN TO BLANKET THE MOUNTAIN.
WE'RE SUPPOSE TO PROVIDE A BLOCKING ACTION ON THE SOUTH SIDE OF THE HILL WHILE BRAVO COMPANY GOES UP THE NORTH SIDE.
YEAH, WELL, FROM THE WAY ALPHA COMPANY CAME BACK DOWN IT LOOKS LIKE THERE WILL BE PLENTY TO GO AROUND.
THERE ALWAYS IS.

AGAIN, COMPANY A CHARGED THE HILL, TOOK A NUMBER OF CASUALTIES, AND WERE FORCED TO WITHDRAW!

ONCE MORE THE BOMBERS AND ARTILLERY POUNDED THE MOUNTAIN FOR HOURS!

AGAIN ALPHA AND BRAVO COMPANIES SURGED UP THE HILL ONLY TO BE BEATEN BACK ONCE MORE!

CAME THE NIGHT.

GOTTA CHECK ON MY PEOPLE, JOURNAL. WE'LL DIG IN HERE 'TIL MORNING.

GO AHEAD. I'LL START THE HOLE.

LOOKS LIKE TOMORROW MORNING IT'S OUR TURN.

DURING THE NIGHT SEVERAL 90mm RECOILLESS RIFLES WERE THROWN INTO THE MIX.

THE MORNING FOUND SFC CRUZ'S PLATOON READY. THEY WOULD TAKE ONE SIDE OF THE HILL WHILE COMPANY A WOULD TAKE THE OTHER. LUCK OF THE DRAW.

GOOD LUCK.

EAT SHIT, GRANDPA!

AT EASE, TROOP.

I ALIGNED MYSELF WITH THE MEDICS AS I HAD AT DAK TO. I ALWAYS FIGURED THAT THOUGH I HAD A TITULAR PRESENCE WITH THE TROOPS I COULD AT LEAST MAKE MYSELF USEFUL IN RETRIEVING THE WOUNDED.

GOING UP THE HILL WOULD ONLY BE HALF THE CHORE. I WATCHED THE YOUNG KIDS SADDLE UP, QUIETLY, THE JOKING AND BITCHING WOULD BE SET ASIDE FOR THE TIME BEING.

IT WAS A DIRTY, THANKLESS, DANGEROUS JOB BUT THEY WOULD DO IT BECAUSE THEY WERE THE SCREAMING EAGLES.

AS THEY STARTED UP THE MOUNTAIN THEY LOOKED YOUNG.

SO VERY YOUNG.

BOTH COMPANIES FOUGHT THEIR WAY TO THE TOP OF THE SADDLEBACK RIDGE THIS TIME...

...AND DESTROYED SEVERAL ENEMY BUNKERS WITH THEIR RECOILLESS RIFLES.

THE SCREAMING EAGLES TRIED TO CONSOLIDATE ON THE RIDGE ... BUT SO DID THE ENEMY...

... AND AGAIN THE GRUNTS LOST THEIR FOOTHOLD AND WERE DRIVEN BACK DOWN THE MOUNTAIN.

THE WOUNDED WERE EVACUATED AND THE NIGHT BROUGHT NO SLEEP FOR THE THIRD NIGHT IN A ROW.

BY MORNING...

ALL THREE COMPANIES ARE DOWN TO HALF STRENGTH. WE AIN'T EVEN MADE A DENT IN THE DINKS DEFENSES.

IT'S SUICIDE TO GO BACK UP THAT HILL.

YEAH, WELL, THAT'S WHAT WE GET COMBAT PAY FOR. IT'S OUR JOB, JOURNAL.

UP UNTIL THEN THE AIR FORCE'S BOMBING HAD LITTLE EFFECT ON THE ENEMY BUNKERS. THEY DECIDED TO TRY SOMETHING NEW, 1000-POUND BOMBS WITH DELAYED FUSES, TO COLLAPSE THE CONNECTING TUNNELS WHICH FED THE SCORES OF UNDERGROUND BUNKERS ALL ALONG THE RIDGE.

HITTING THE THIN RAZORBACK PROVED TO BE MORE DIFFICULT THAN THE PILOTS HAD EXPECTED...

...HOWEVER, A FEW DOZEN FOUND THEIR MARKS...

...AND THE ENTIRE RIDGE COLLAPSED.

RRRUUMMBBLLLEEE

SECONDARY EXPLOSIONS RIPPED GIANT HOLES IN THE SCARED MOUNTAIN.

BUT UNLIKE SO MANY TIMES BEFORE THE NORTH VIETNAMESE HAD NO INTENTION OF ABANDONING THEIR POSITIONS, THEY FULLY INTENDED TO FIGHT TO THE LAST MAN.

THE BATTLE WAS FAR FROM OVER. THREE TIMES THAT MORNING THE BOYS OF THE 502nd TRIED AGAIN TO REACH THE SUMMIT AND WERE DRIVEN BACK.

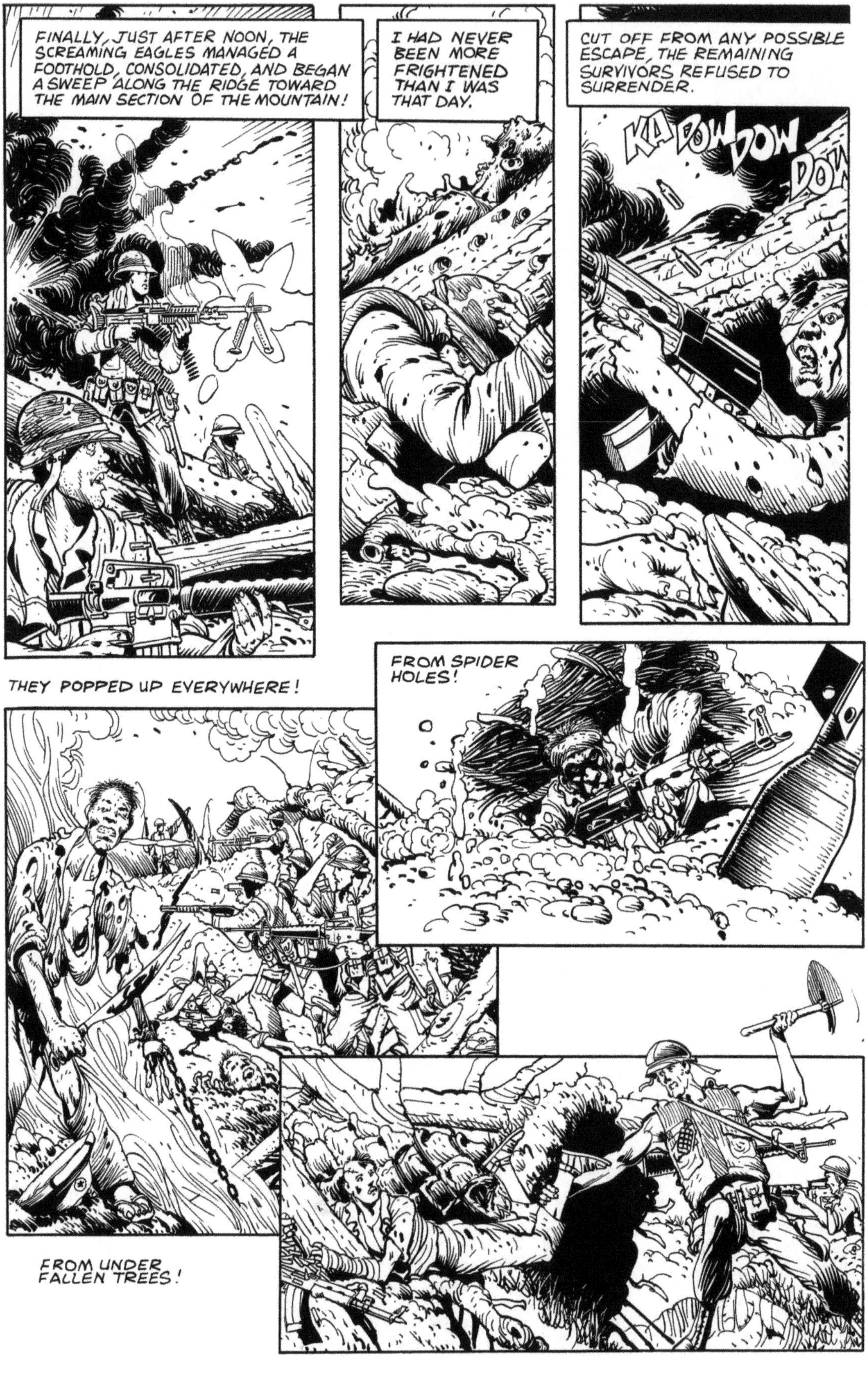
FINALLY, JUST AFTER NOON, THE SCREAMING EAGLES MANAGED A FOOTHOLD, CONSOLIDATED, AND BEGAN A SWEEP ALONG THE RIDGE TOWARD THE MAIN SECTION OF THE MOUNTAIN!
I HAD NEVER BEEN MORE FRIGHTENED THAN I WAS THAT DAY.
CUT OFF FROM ANY POSSIBLE ESCAPE, THE REMAINING SURVIVORS REFUSED TO SURRENDER.
KADOW DOW DOW
THEY POPPED UP EVERYWHERE!
FROM SPIDER HOLES!
FROM UNDER FALLEN TREES!

AND IN COLLAPSED BUNKERS UNDER PILES OF THEIR CRISP-FRIED COMRADS.

BUT IT WAS NO TURKEY SHOOT. I LAID BACK, I'M A LITTLE ASHAMED TO SAY. AFTER NEARLY A WEEK OF DIARRHEA MY STOMACH WAS CHURNING AND MY LEGS WOBBLY.

THEN A LITTLE REALITY CHECK. THERE WAS NO SAFE PLACE ON "BLOODY RIDGE" THAT DAY!

THE HEAVY SLUG SPLINTERED WOOD ONLY AN INCH FROM MY HEAD!

THEN I SAW HIM... OR WHAT WAS LEFT OF HIM.

KA-DOW

SMAT

JUDAS PRIEST!

I WAS TRAPPED! MY ONLY ESCAPE WAS PAST HIM! MAYBE THIS WAS IT. MAYBE THIS WAS THE WAY IT WOULD END FOR ME. MAYBE I HAD PUSHED MY LUCK ONE TOO MANY TIMES.

MAYBE NOT.

CLICK

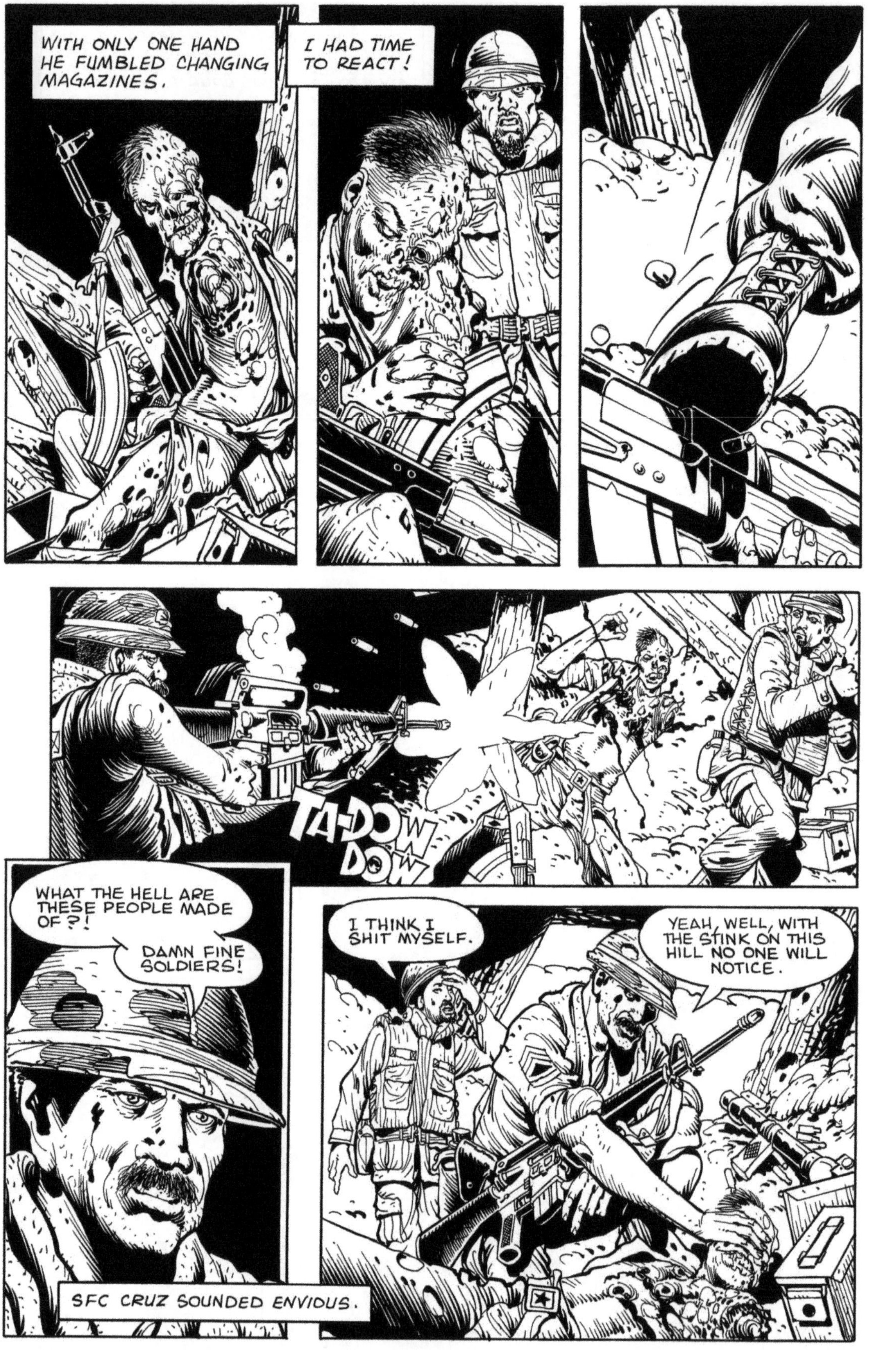
WITH ONLY ONE HAND HE FUMBLED CHANGING MAGAZINES.
I HAD TIME TO REACT!
TA-DOW DOW
WHAT THE HELL ARE THESE PEOPLE MADE OF?!
DAMN FINE SOLDIERS!
SFC CRUZ SOUNDED ENVIOUS.
I THINK I SHIT MYSELF.
YEAH, WELL, WITH THE STINK ON THIS HILL NO ONE WILL NOTICE.

ON THE MOUNTAIN PROPER, DEVASTATION AND THE SMELL OF DEATH WAS EVERYWHERE.

HEY, OLD GUY, YOU'RE THE REPORTER, RIGHT?

HUH? OH, YEAH.

ON THE SOUTH SIDE OF THE MOUNTAIN WE FOUND A HOSPITAL, LOTS OF DEAD DINKS...

AND SOMETHING ELSE, WE FOUND THIS WITH THE MEDICAL SUPPLIES.

I FELT THE HEAT ROLL UP FROM DEEP DOWN INSIDE ME.

IT WAS AN INVENTORY FOR MEDICAL SUPPLIES DONATED TO THE COMMUNISTS. AT THE BOTTOM IT READ, "DONATED BY YOUR FRIENDS AT THE UNIVERSITY OF CALIFORNIA AT BERKELEY."

FUCK!

I DID NOT TAKE IT AS A PERSONAL INSULT. I DID NOT HAVE THE RIGHT. BUT IT **WAS** A PERSONAL INSULT TO EVERY BRAVE YOUNG MAN WHO HAD FOUGHT AND DIED ON THAT STINKING HILL. I FELT VERY ALONE.

I COULD ONLY IMAGINE HOW THE TROOPS FELT.

Missing American

SSgt. Raymond G. Czerwiec and SP4. Clarence A. Latimer 4th Infantry troopers left behind during heated battle

The following profiles two of those Missing Americans.

On March 27, 1969, SSgt. Raymond Czerwiec and SP4 Clarence Latimer were rifleman with Company A, 3rd Battalion, 12th Infantry and on a reconnaissance Mission in Kontum Province, South Vietnam when their platoon came under hostile weapons fire and were forced to withdraw with a number of people missing.

An attempt to re-enter the area that afternoon was unsuccessful, Another attempt was made on the 28th but it too was unsuccessful. Air strikes and artillery fire were placed into the enemy area for two days.

On March 30, Company A attacked the enemy again, and was again forced to withdraw, leaving people behind, including SP4 Clarence A. Latimer, who was a rifleman with the company and had been severely wounded during the attempt.

Two long range Reconnaissance patrols (LRRP) awere sent into the area a week later to recover the bodies of the missing. Sweeps were made of the area for two days, but no remains were found. Clarence A. Latimer was declared Missing In Action.

On March 3, 1973, a fellow 4th Inf. trooper Gail Kerns was released by the North Vietnamese having been captured in the same area. Kerns was unconscious when captured and did not know the fate of SSgt. Raymond G. Czerwiec or SP4 Clarence A. Latimer.

CZERWIEC, RAYMOND GEORGE	LATIMER, CLARENCE ALBERT
Raymond George Czerwiec	Clarence Albert Latimer
Staff Sergeant/US Army	Sergeant First Class/US Army
Company A, 3rd Battalion, 12th Infantry, 4th Infantry Division	Company A, 3rd Battalion, 12th Infantry, 4th Infantry Division
21 February 1944	27 August 1947 (Charlotte, NC)
Chicago, IL	Due West, SC
27 March 1969	27 March 1969
South Vietnam	South Vietnam

Since the end of the Vietnam War there have been more than 21,000 reports received by our government about American prisoners, missing, and otherwise unaccounted for personnel. Many of these reports were from actual eye witnesses in the Southeast Asian theater and document LIVE Americans being held captive even today. How long will we allow this tragedy to continue?

American servicemen served selflessly and in harm's way in the decade long struggle in Southeast Asia to include Vietnam, Laos, Cambodia, and Thailand, were wounded, taken prisoner, and killed as witnessed by the 58,000 names on the black slab wall of remembrance in Washington D.C. Every missing fighting man who served in the Vietnam War deserves to be accounted for. America has always taken pride in leaving no fighting man behind. What can you do? Educate yourself on this subject.

Vietnam Journal
Valley of
DEATH

INFIL...

Vietnam Journal™
Valley of DEATH™

INFIL...

Story & Art DON LOMAX

I LEFT THE HILL (BLOODY RIDGE) AND DID NOT LOOK BACK. I DID NOT EVEN SAY MY "GOOD-BYES" TO SFC CRUZ AND THE OTHER BATTLE DECIMATED TROOPS OF THE 101ST IN MY DESPERATE SEARCH FOR A BOTTLE TO CRAWL INTO.

BUT THIS TIME IT WAS DIFFERENT. THIS TIME MY OLD FRIEND, BOOZE, LET ME DOWN. I DID NOT FORGET THE HORROR OF THAT HILL OR THE PAIN OF THE MISGUIDED CHILDREN, AND MOST OF THEM WERE JUST KIDS, WHO FOUGHT AND DIED THERE FOR NO GOOD REASON THAT I COULD DETERMINE. THIS TIME IT ONLY MADE IT WORSE TO THE POINT THAT AFTER A THREE DAY BINGE I SWORE MY DRINKING DAYS WERE OVER. I SWORE OFF BOOZE... FOR THE THIRD TIME THIS YEAR AND IT WAS ONLY LATE APRIL.

1969 WAS A PEAK YEAR OF SWEARING OFF BOOZE FOR ME.

THE TIMES! NO SHIT, CAN I READ THAT WHEN YOU'RE FINISHED?

HUH? OH, YEAH, YOU CAN HAVE IT... SOMEONE GAVE IT TO ME.

SO THAT'S NIXON'S "SECRET PLAN TO END THE WAR"? THE ONE THAT GOT HIM ELECTED? TURN IT ALL OVER TO "MARVIN" AND DI DI MOW BEFORE THE WHOLE SHITFACED HOUSE OF CARDS COMES CRASHING DOWN AROUND THEIR EARS?

A-FIRMATIVE. SEC. HAIG CALLS IT "VIETNAMIZATION".

SO WHAT'S YOUR FUNCTION HERE AT THE JUNCTION, YOUNG TROOPER?

HUH? OH... I'M HERE TO PICK UP ANOTHER NEW SHAVETAIL REPLACEMENT FOR OUR COMPANY. WE GO THROUGH A SHIT-LOAD OF LIEUTENANTS WHERE I'M FROM.

I SWARE TO GOD, THESE LITTLE GIRLS LOOK YOUNGER EVERY TIME I COME TO TOWN.

OLD ENOUGH TO BLEED, OLD ENOUGH TO BREED. AIN'T THAT RIGHT? HUH, AIN'T IT?

REMIND ME TO BUST THAT SON-OF-A-BITCHE'S HEAD OPEN ON MY WAY OUT.

ANYWAY, YOU WERE SAYING?

OH, YEAH, I'M COMPANY CLERK FOR A LITTLE TURD OF A FIREBASE A FEW KLICKS UP THE VALLEY...

"THE TROOPS BLAMED LIEUTENANT DUMBSHIT, A 90 DAY WONDER JUST IN FROM 'HAPPYLAND' AS A REPLACEMENT FOR THEIR MUCH BELOVED, AND MUCH DEAD, ROTC PLATOON LEADER WHOM THEY HAD PERSONALLY TAGGED AND BAGGED, SENDING HIS REMAINS HOME TO HIS LOVING MOMMY."

THERE IT IS.

SAND PACKERS

FUCKIN'-A.

"WE TOLD THE 'FRESH MEAT' LIEUTENANT ABOUT THE DANGER SPOT IN OUR PERIMETER, A DRAINAGE CULVERT THAT LED UNDER THE WIRE AND INTO OUR COMPOUND."

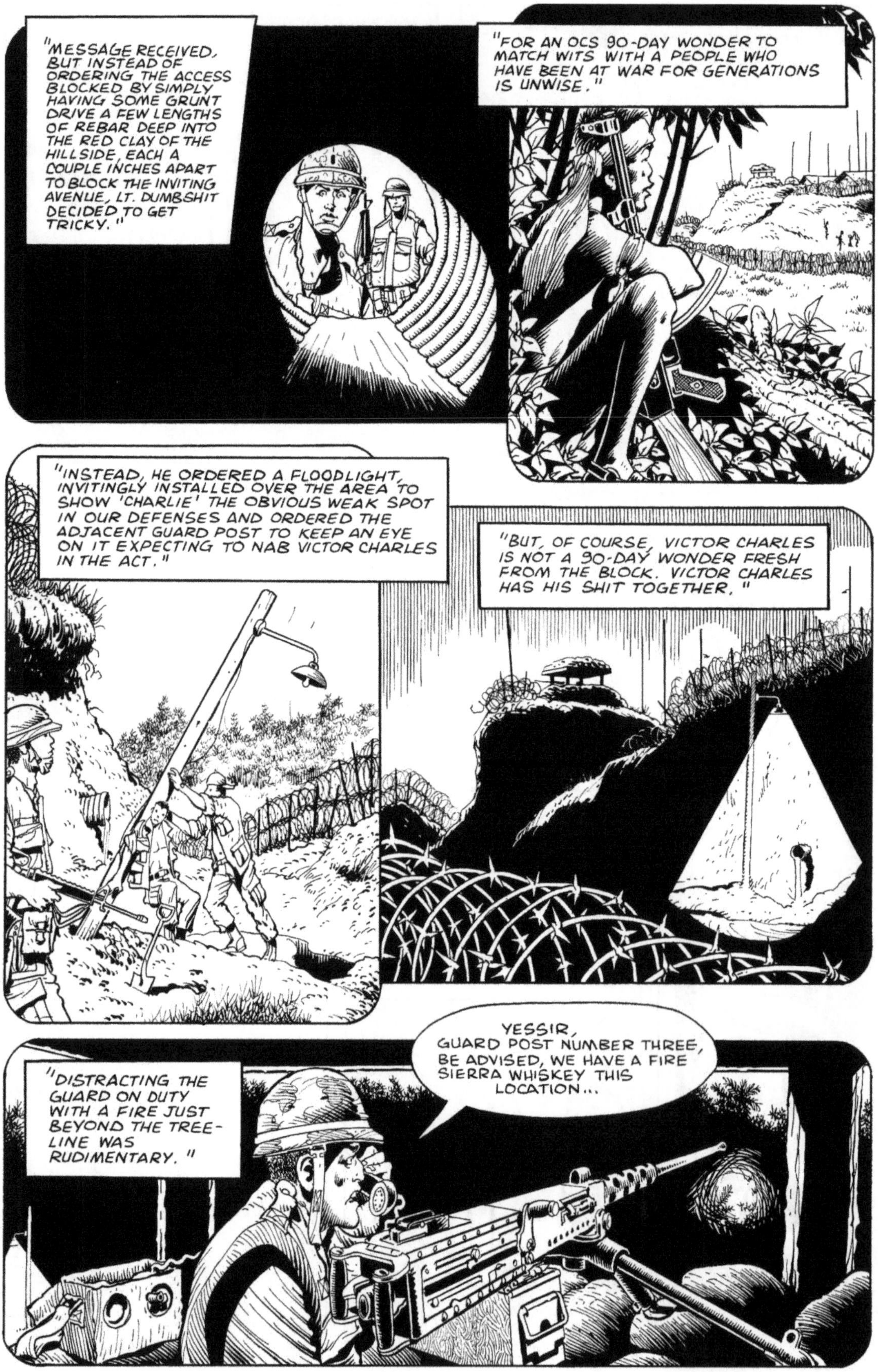
"MESSAGE RECEIVED, BUT INSTEAD OF ORDERING THE ACCESS BLOCKED BY SIMPLY HAVING SOME GRUNT DRIVE A FEW LENGTHS OF REBAR DEEP INTO THE RED CLAY OF THE HILLSIDE, EACH A COUPLE INCHES APART TO BLOCK THE INVITING AVENUE, LT. DUMBSHIT DECIDED TO GET TRICKY."
"FOR AN OCS 90-DAY WONDER TO MATCH WITS WITH A PEOPLE WHO HAVE BEEN AT WAR FOR GENERATIONS IS UNWISE."
"INSTEAD, HE ORDERED A FLOODLIGHT, INVITINGLY INSTALLED OVER THE AREA TO SHOW 'CHARLIE' THE OBVIOUS WEAK SPOT IN OUR DEFENSES AND ORDERED THE ADJACENT GUARD POST TO KEEP AN EYE ON IT EXPECTING TO NAB VICTOR CHARLES IN THE ACT."
"BUT, OF COURSE, VICTOR CHARLES IS NOT A 90-DAY WONDER FRESH FROM THE BLOCK. VICTOR CHARLES HAS HIS SHIT TOGETHER."
"DISTRACTING THE GUARD ON DUTY WITH A FIRE JUST BEYOND THE TREE-LINE WAS RUDIMENTARY."
YESSIR, GUARD POST NUMBER THREE, BE ADVISED, WE HAVE A FIRE SIERRA WHISKEY THIS LOCATION...

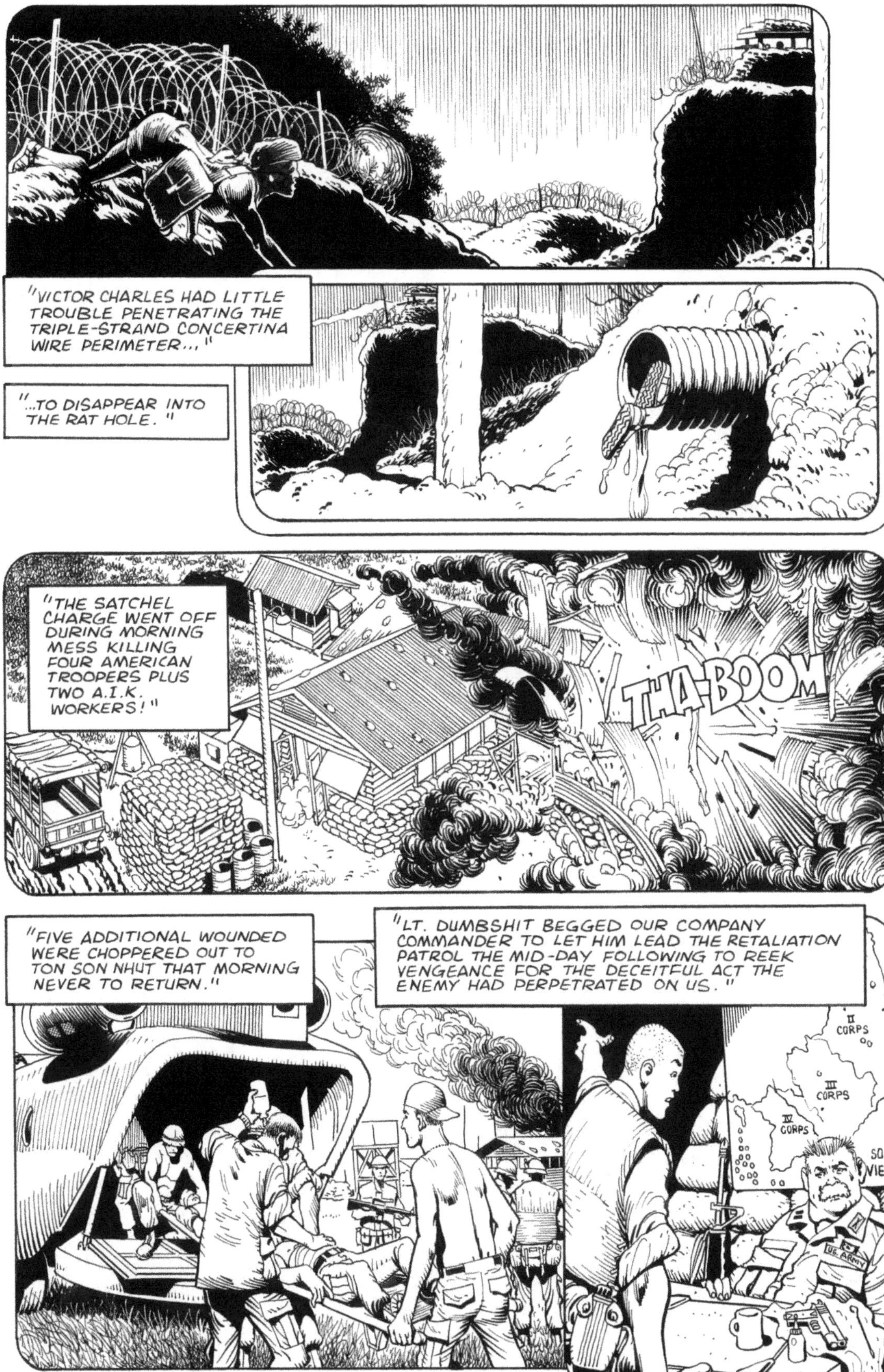

"VICTOR CHARLES HAD LITTLE TROUBLE PENETRATING THE TRIPLE-STRAND CONCERTINA WIRE PERIMETER..."
"...TO DISAPPEAR INTO THE RAT HOLE."
"THE SATCHEL CHARGE WENT OFF DURING MORNING MESS KILLING FOUR AMERICAN TROOPERS PLUS TWO A.I.K. WORKERS!"
THA-BOOM
"FIVE ADDITIONAL WOUNDED WERE CHOPPERED OUT TO TON SON NHUT THAT MORNING NEVER TO RETURN."
"LT. DUMBSHIT BEGGED OUR COMPANY COMMANDER TO LET HIM LEAD THE RETALIATION PATROL THE MID-DAY FOLLOWING TO REEK VENGEANCE FOR THE DECEITFUL ACT THE ENEMY HAD PERPETRATED ON US."
II CORPS
III CORPS
IV CORPS
US. ARMY

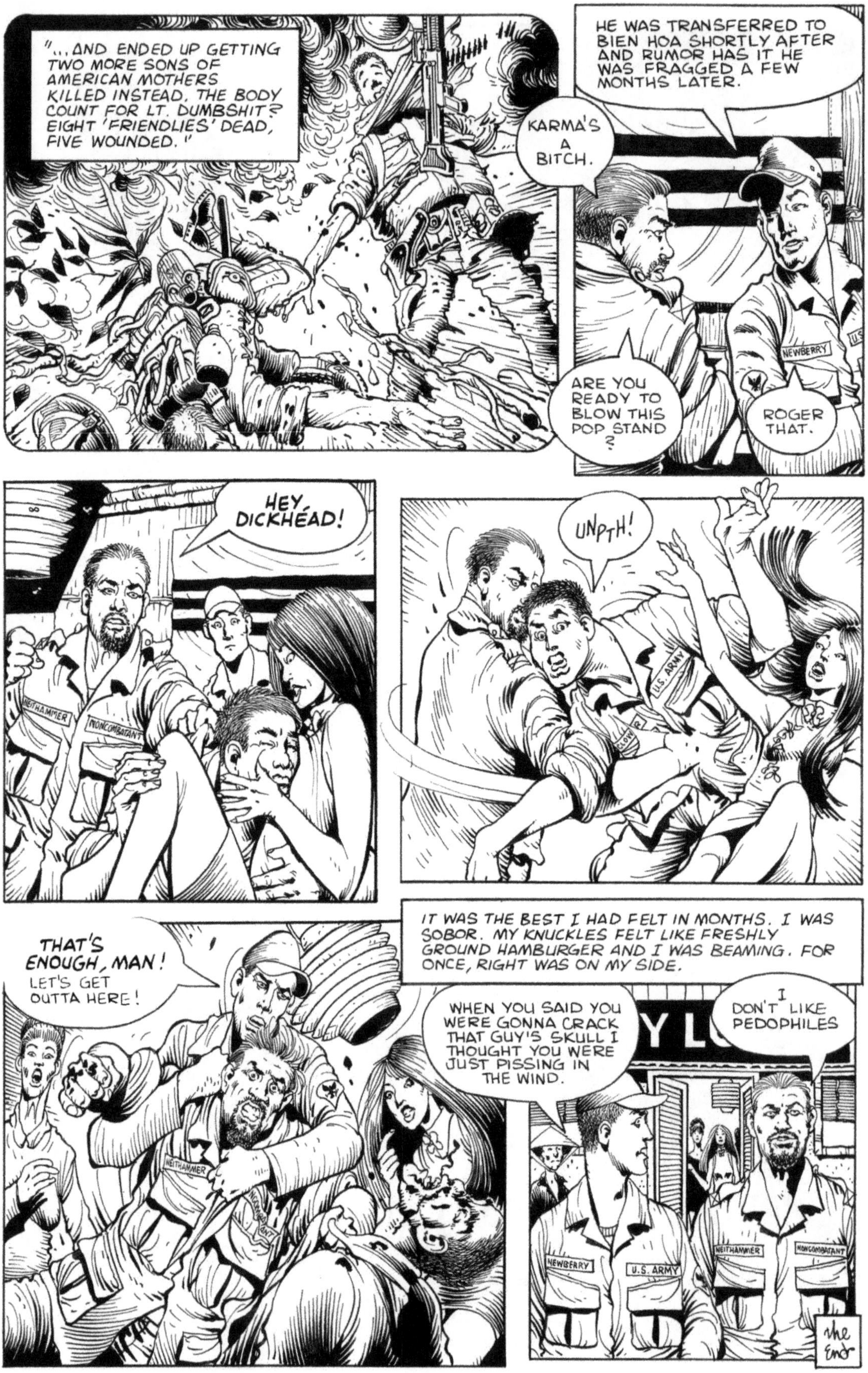
"... AND ENDED UP GETTING TWO MORE SONS OF AMERICAN MOTHERS KILLED INSTEAD. THE BODY COUNT FOR LT. DUMBSHIT? EIGHT 'FRIENDLIES' DEAD, FIVE WOUNDED."
HE WAS TRANSFERRED TO BIEN HOA SHORTLY AFTER AND RUMOR HAS IT HE WAS FRAGGED A FEW MONTHS LATER.
KARMA'S A BITCH.
NEWBERRY
ARE YOU READY TO BLOW THIS POP STAND?
ROGER THAT.
HEY, DICKHEAD!
NEITHAMMER
NONCOMBATANT
UNPTH!
U.S. ARMY
THAT'S ENOUGH, MAN! LET'S GET OUTTA HERE!
NEITHAMMER
IT WAS THE BEST I HAD FELT IN MONTHS. I WAS SOBOR. MY KNUCKLES FELT LIKE FRESHLY GROUND HAMBURGER AND I WAS BEAMING. FOR ONCE, RIGHT WAS ON MY SIDE.
WHEN YOU SAID YOU WERE GONNA CRACK THAT GUY'S SKULL I THOUGHT YOU WERE JUST PISSING IN THE WIND.
I DON'T LIKE PEDOPHILES
NEWBERRY
U.S. ARMY
NEITHAMMER
NONCOMBATANT
the End

Missing American

Reports have SFC James Salley and SP4 Phillip Terrill dead and buried in Laos near the Ho Chi Minh Trail but no remains have been returned. Their families deserve better.

The following profiles two of those Missing Americans;

SFC James Salley Jr., an advisor from Advance Team 22, MACV, and SP4 Phillip Terrill, a rifleman from HHB, 1st Battalion, 92nd Artillery were part of an integrated observation systems team and were taken captive together on March 31, 1971 after fire support base Number 6 on Hill 1001 was overrun by elements of the 66th NVA Regiment. The support base, including an ARVN camp, was located in Kontum Province, South Vietnam.

Liberation Radio and Hanoi Radio broadcasts in early April 1971 and a Quan Doi Nhan Dan article appearing in July 1972 referred to this battle and the capture of the American advisors.

In 1973, 591 American prisoners were released, but Terrill and Salley were not among them. Sgt. David F. Allwine, who was released, stated that he had been held with SFC Salley in captivity when Sally died on July 15, 1971. He also said that he had helped bury SFC Salley in Laos at the POW camp. According to Allwine, Salley told him that SP4 Terrell, who had been seriously wounded, had died on the trail only four days after his capture.

SFC Salley's death was officially acknowledged in January 1973 by the Provisional Revolutionary Government (PRG) of South Vietnam, with his date of death given as August 15. 1971. The PRG, however, never acknowledged SP4 Terrill's death, nor has Vietnam returned either of the two men's bodies.

SALLEY, JAMES JR.	TERRILL, PHILIP BRADFORD
James Salley, Jr. Master Sergeant/US Army Advisory Team 22, MACV 17 August 1930 (Denmark, SC) Columbia, SC 31 March 1971 South Vietnam 	Philip Bradford Terrill Specialist 5th Class/US Army Headquarter and Headquarters Battery 1st Battalion, 92nd Artillery 24 September 1947 (Utica, NY) Hartford, NY 31 March 1971 South Vietnam 

Since the end of the Vietnam War there have been more than 21,000 reports received by our government about American prisoners, missing, and otherwise unaccounted for personnel. Many of these reports were from actual eye witnesses in the Southeast Asian theater and document LIVE Americans being held captive even today. How long will we allow this tragedy to continue?

American servicemen served selflessly and in harm's way in the decade long struggle in Southeast Asia to include Vietnam, Laos, Cambodia, and Thailand, were wounded, taken prisoner, and killed as witnessed by the 58,000 names on the black slab wall of remembrance in Washington D.C. Every missing fighting man who served in the Vietnam War deserves to be accounted for. America has always taken pride in leaving no fighting man behind. What can you do? Educate yourself on this subject.

HAMBURGER
HILL

The following pages are from
VIETNAM JOURNAL: HAMBURGER HILL
that originally appeared in Gallery Magazine
as an on-going single page serial

VIETNAM JOURNAL

by Don Lomax

JOURNALISTS IN VIETNAM ENJOYED REMARKABLE FREEDOM REPORTING ON THE WAR. MACV SELDOM OBJECTED TO OUR MOVEMENT IN ANY AREA OF OPERATION. IF I COULD BUM A RIDE I COULD GET MY ASS IN THE GRASS WITH THE GRUNTS. BUT SOMETIMES THE TAXI RIDE THERE WAS MORE TEDIOUS THAN THE MISSION. MY NAME'S SCOTT NEITHAMMER...

THE TROOPS CALL ME 'JOURNAL'.

THE PUCKER FACTOR ON THIS PARTICULAR MISSION WAS A STRONG *NUMBA-TEN*.

KEEP YOUR ASS-CHEEKS WIRED TIGHT, OLD-TIMER. WE'RE COMING IN HOT. STICK WITH ME LIKE I'M YOUR VIRGINAL PROM DATE AND I'LL GET YOU THROUGH.

MODERN JOURNALISTS SALIVATE WHEN THEY HEAR OF THE FREEDOM OF MOVEMENT CORRESPONDENTS ENJOYED IN VIETNAM.

BACK AT MACV THEY SAID THIS A.O. WAS NOTHING BUT FRIENDLY!

THAT'S RIGHT, JOURNAL. THOSE ARE JUST FRIENDLY BEES ZIPPING PAST YOUR EARS.

AN UNCENSORED IMPUNITY THAT SOME HISTORIANS BLAME FOR THE LOSS OF THE WAR. BUT IT WAS NOT THE PRESS OR THE AMERICAN FIGHTING MAN WHO LOST THE WAR.

IT WAS SINGLE-MINDED POLITICIANS AND THEIR JOINT CHIEFS ENGAGED IN DECADES LONG ORGIES OF SAVE-YOUR-OWN-ASS CLUSTERFUCKS THAT LEFT A LEGACY OF GUILT AND MISTRUST OF THE GOVERNMENT...

RPG! STARBOARD! FUCKING RPG!

...DRAGGING AN ENTIRE GENERATION OF AMERICANS THROUGH DECADES OF SKEPTICISM AND POLITICAL EMBARRASSMENT.

CHARLIE 2-6, WE'VE TAKEN A ROCKET! THE HYDRAULICS ARE OUT... WE'RE GOING IN!

OH, SHIT!

DOUBLE SHIT!

TA-BOOM

THE AN LAO VALLEY, SEPTEMBER 1967, A CORDON-AND-SEARCH MISSION FOR INTERDICTION OF VIET CONG FORCES. BUT THE TROOPS HAD MORE COLORFUL TERMINOLOGY...

BROWSE AND BUTCHER...

FLUSH AND FRAG.

SMAT SMAT SMAT SMAT

CHARLIE 2-6 IS DOWN... SCOUTS CONGREGATE ON THE CRASH SIGHT AND SECURE!

A-FIRM, DEVIL-DOG!

I WAS SLAMMED TO THE METAL DECK AS THE SLICK BELLIED OUT IN THE PADDY, ITS BROAD, MAIN ROTOR SLICING INTO THE MUD, SENDING A TORRENT OF SPRAY 100 FEET INTO THE AIR.

MY EARS WERE RINGING. THE SMELL OF AVIATION FUEL BURNED MY NOSTRILS.

COME ON, JOURNAL, MOVE IT! HE'S DEAD!

THE TREE-LINE... NOVEMBER WHISKEY! GIVE 'EM HELL, HAWKS!

HERE! TAKE COVER THIS IS A GOOD PLACE TO WATCH THE SHOW!

I CAN'T SEE! I'VE GOT MUD IN MY EYES!

I HATE TO BE THE ONE TO BREAK IT TO YOU, JOURNAL... THAT AIN'T MUD!

YEAH, IT'S BUFFALO SHIT, OLD-TIMER.

CONTINUED...

VIETNAM JOURNAL

by Don Lomax

PAINFUL LESSONS LEARNED BY THE FIRST AIR CAVALRY IN THE BATTLE FOR THE IA DRANG VALLEY IN 1965 HAD TAUGHT THE BRASS TO RESIST DEPLOYING ALL THEIR FORCES TO ANY THEATER OF HEAVY ENEMY PRESENCE. A BATTALION STRENGTH READY REACTION FORCE (RRF) HELD IN RESERVE WAS CREATED TO ENGAGE THE VIET CONG, COMPANY STRENGTH, IN A MATTER OF MOMENTS.

BY SEPTEMBER OF 1967 THE COSTAL CAMPAIGN OF THE FIRST CAVALRY FOCUSED ON THE HEAVILY POPULATED BONG SON PLAINS. OUR MISSION WAS JUST ONE OF MANY EXTRACTING A HEAVY TOLL ON MEN AND EQUIPMENT CAUSING THE AIRCRAFT TO BE REPLACED TWICE OVER.

THE "WHITE" SCOUT HELICOPTERS WOULD INITIATE FIRST CONTACT MAKING A TEMPTING TARGET THE ENEMY COULD NOT RESIST.

THEN THE "RED" TEAMS JOIN THE FRAY WITH THEIR "HEAVY HOGS"... WEAPONS LADEN HUEYS WITH A CHIP ON THEIR SHOULDERS.

DUST OFF'S COMIN' IN. GET YERSELF ON THIS CHOPPER WITH THE WOUNDED.

FOLLOWED, FINALLY, BY THE "BLUE" TEAMS... SLICKS WITH AIR DELIVERED RIFLE PLATOONS GEARED TO HIT THE GROUND RUNNING AND BRING A WORLD OF HURT TO ANY UNFORTUNATE ENEMY.

BUT...

THE STORY IS HERE, JOURNAL. I'LL BET MY LEFT NUT CHARLIE'S ALREADY GONE.

JUST AS OFTEN THE ENEMY WOULD SIMPLY DISOLVE INTO THEIR HIDDEN STRONGHOLDS IN THE MOUNTIANS TO THE WEST. 'NAM WAS A LONG, PROTRACTED WAR.

KEEP YER HEAD DOWN, OLD TIMER. I GOT A FEELIN' THERE'S PEOPLE AROUND HERE WHO DON'T LIKE US.

NO SHIT?

THAT'S THE WAY IT WAS. LIKE THEY SAY, A LION CAN BRING DOWN AN ELEPHANT IF HE BITES IT ONCE A DAY. VIETNAM WAS BLEEDING FROM SELF-INFLICTED WOUNDS.

CONTINUED...

VIETNAM JOURNAL

by Don Lomax

1967: THE SUMMER OF LOVE.
THE TROOPS IN VIETNAM DID NOT GET THE MEMO. THEIR'S WAS A DIFFERENT ARMY THAN THAT OF TODAY... DRAFTEES. MANY DELINQUENT TEEN- AGERS WHO'S HOMETOWN JUDGES, IN COLLUSION WITH LOCAL DRAFTBOARDS, GAVE MANY A MISGUIDED YOUTH THE CHOICE OF JAIL OR VIETNAM. IT WAS OFTEN A DEATH SENTENCE FOR A PETTY RUN-IN WITH THE LAW.

FOR THOSE SAME POLITICIANS' AND MAYORS' SONS, DODGING THE DRAFT WAS A SIMPLE CASE OF COLLEGE DEFERMENT OR A MUCH PRIZED POSITION IN THE NATIONAL GUARD. IT WAS A POOR, UNEDUCATED BOYS WAR. NO SENATOR'S SON DIED IN VIETNAM.

THE ORDERLY ROOM'S THAT WAY, JOURNAL... GOOD LUCK WITH THE FIRST SHIRT. HE'S A 24 KARAT GOLD NUT-BUSTER.

I GOT THE WORD IN SAIGON. I HAD BEST GET PERMISSION FROM THE FIRST SERGEANT IF I WANTED TO ACCOMPANY ONE OF HIS LARPS INTO THE BOONIES. IT WAS LIKE PULLING TEETH. HE DID NOT LIKE THE PRESS MUCH.

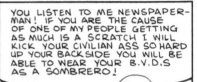

YOU LISTEN TO ME NEWSPAPER- MAN! IF YOU ARE THE CAUSE OF ONE OF MY PEOPLE GETTING AS MUCH IS A SCRATCH I WILL KICK YOUR CIVILIAN ASS SO HARD UP YOUR BACKSIDE YOU WILL BE ABLE TO WEAR YOUR B.V.D.S AS A SOMBRERO!

I BELIEVED HIM. THIRD ROW, TENT FOUR. I HATED TO WAKE THEM BUT I DID NOT HAVE A CHOICE IF I WAS GOING TO CHOPPER OUT OF THERE WITH THEM AT 05:00.

A... HELLO?

MY NAMES SCOTT NEITHAMMER! I COME IN PEACE...

WELL, YOU DAMN NEAR ENDED UP IN PIECES.

THAT'S THE NEWSPAPER GUY... HE WANTS TO GET CLOSE TO "CHUCK".

DON'T YOU WORRY, DICKBREATH... WE'LL GET YOU CLOSE ENOUGH TO CHARLIE TO GIVE HIM TONGUE, IF YOU BE SO INCLINED.

FUCKIN' A- FIRMA- TIVE!

CONTINUED...

VIETNAM JOURNAL

by Don Lomax

CONTINUED ...

LONG RANGE RECONNAISSANCE PATROL (*LIRPS*). HELICOPTER INSERTED AND NOISE DISCIPLINED, THEIR PRIMARY TASK WAS GATHERING INTELLIGENCE.

CONTACT WITH THE ENEMY WAS AVOIDED AND WHEN THE ENEMY WAS SPOTTED THEIR JOB WAS TO CALL IN ARTILLERY ON THE BAD GUYS AND HOTEL ALPHA (*HAUL ASS*) FOR EXTRACTION BY CHOPPER. IN THE IDEAL MISSION THE ENEMY WOULD NEVER EVEN KNOW THEY HAD BEEN THERE. BUT THERE WERE FEW THINGS IDEAL IN VIETNAM.

SUMMER, 1967. IT WAS HOTTER THAN A FRESH FUCKED FOX IN A FOREST FIRE WHEN WE WERE DROPPED OFF IN THE THICK JUNGLE NEAR THE CAMBODIAN BORDER.

THE TEAM LEADER, LT. MITCHELL... QUIET CONFIDENCE, DID NOT MUCH APPRECIATE ME BEING ALONG.

PFC GOMEZ, THE RADIOMAN,

AND THE TAIL-GUNNER, SPEC-4 PEAL MADE UP THE TEAM.

CORPORAL COSTELLO, THE POINT MAN... I COULD TELL, THE SHORT TIME I HAD KNOWN HIM, HE DID NOT MISS MUCH.

I'M SCOTT NEITHAMMER, THE TROOPS CALL ME 'JOURNAL'. WE CAME UPON A HAMLET. I COULD TELL IT WAS UNEXPECTED.

SHE'S ZONED OUT, MAN.

THE OLD WOMAN WAS HOLDING THE BABY TIGHTLY, STARING INTO SPACE.

I'LL GET THE BABY.

OH, GOD!

OH, MY GOD!

THE VIET CONG DID THIS?

ROGER THAT.

BUT WHAT DO THEY ACCOMPLISH BY BUTCHERING EVERYONE IN THE VILLAGE.

IT'S NOT ABOUT THIS VILLE... IT'S A MESSAGE FOR THE NEXT ONE. AND YOU CAN BET WHEN CHARLIE SAYS 'FROG' THEY'RE GONNA JUMP.

CONTINUED ...

VIETNAM JOURNAL

by Don Lomax

53 BUTCHERED CIVILIANS. THE REST OF THE VILLAGERS HAD APPARENTLY EVAPORATED INTO THE JUNGLE. SADLY, IT WOULD HARDLY BE A FOOTNOTE IN THIS CONVOLUTED WASTE OF A WAR.

DULY NOTED... IT WAS ALL WE COULD DO. WE PREPARED TO MOVE ON.

YOU TRAVEL LIGHT FOR A CIVILIAN. THIS AIN'T YOUR FIRST WAR.

NAW, KOREA.

JUST ONE THING. YOU'D BEST DROP THAT FLACK JACKET IN THE WELL OR YOU'RE GONNA HAVE A STROKE, JOURNAL.

IT WAS GOOD ADVICE. BACK TO SPEAKING WITH HAND SIGNALS. THE JUNGLE AIR LAID ON US LIKE DAMP BURLAP. IT WAS A STRUGGLE JUST TO BREATH.

AND THE NIGHTS? DAMNEDEST, MOST MISERABLE, TERRIFYING NIGHTS I HAD EVER IMAGINED. EVERY SHADOW WAS A WILD-EYED VIET CONG SQUATTING AT WAIT FOR HIS CHANCE AT ME.

THOUGH THERE WAS NO INDICATION OF A BORDER, I HAD A FEELING WE WERE IN CAMBODIA AS WE DOGGED THE FAMOUS HO CHI MINH TRAIL.

IT WAS OUR CONSTANT ATTEMPT TO INTERDICT AND STEM THE FLOOD OF WEAPONS AND AMMUNITION FROM NORTH VIETNAM INTO THE SOUTH. WITHOUT CONSTANT RESUPPLY THE VIET CONG WOULD WITHER ON THE VINE.

THEY CALLED IT "ROLLING THUNDER". I WAS SOON TO UNDERSTAND WHY.

CONTINUED...

VIETNAM JOURNAL

by Don Lomax

IT WAS TIME TO HITCH HIPS AND HOTEL ALPHA. WE WERE OUT OF THE TARGET AREA WHEN THE GROUND ROLLED UNDER US LIKE SWELLS ON THE OCEAN. THE EARTH ACTUALLY ROSE AND FELL WITH EACH SORTIE OF BOMBS.

THEN THE SYMPHONY OF MUFFLED THUDS SEEMED TO GO ON FOREVER. "ROLLING THUNDER"

...APTLY NAMED.

I COULD ONLY IMAGINE THE HORROR OF BEING ON THE RECEIVING END OF SUCH A B-52 STRIKE.

TOTAL ANNIHILATION.

OUR TAXI RIDE BACK TO BASE WAS ALREADY ON ITS WAY TO PICK US UP, BUT THE EXTRACTION POINT WAS STILL A FEW "KLICKS" AWAY. WE WERE MOVING AS FAST AS WE COULD AND STILL MAINTAIN A MEASURE OF SECURITY. THE AIR WAS SATURATED ...HARD TO BREATH.

MOVE YER ASS, OLD MAN, OR WE'LL LEAVE YOU FER "CHARLIE".

THEY WOULD... AND THEY SHOULD. IT WAS OUR AGREEMENT IF I COULD NOT KEEP UP.

THEN...

AW, SHIT! LOOK AT THAT!

AN AMERICAN AIRMAN.

IT LOOKED LIKE HE HAD BEEN HANGING THERE FOR MONTHS.

SKIPPER! WE GOT A PATROL COMIN'! LOOKS LIKE HALF A DOZEN DINKS AND SOME ARVN PRISONERS.

DAMN... FIND A SPOT, GO TO GROUND! WE DON'T HAVE TIME TO EVADE.

COME ON, JOURNAL... TAKE COVER IN THAT MANGROVE. IT LOOKS LIKE OUR RECORD FOR NEGATIVE CONTACT IS JUST ABOUT TO BE BROKEN.

THE LIEUTENANT SEEMED STRANGELY CALM. I TOOK THE AIRMAN'S TAGS... I WOULD TURN THEM IN...

IF WE LIVED.

CONTINUED...

VIETNAM JOURNAL

by Don Lomax

THE COLUMN OF VIET CONG APPROACHED OUR CONCEALMENT MOVING RAPIDLY AWAY FROM THE SATURATION BOMBING. MY BLOOD POUNDED IN MY EARS. SURELY THEY WOULD DISCOVER US. MY DRUMLIKE HEARTBEAT ALONE SHOULD BE ENOUGH TO GIVE US AWAY.

THE PRISONERS, HALF DEAD FROM TORTURE, STRUGGLED TO MAINTAIN THE PACE. MY LARP COMRADS HAD DISOLVED INTO THE JUNGLE. I HAD NEVER FELT SO ALONE.

AT ANY SECOND I EXPECTED THE ENTIRE JUNGLE WOULD ERUPT IN AN INTENSE FIRE-FIGHT. BUT ONLY THE MUFFLED SOUNDS OF SANDALS FADING INTO THE UNDERGROWTH WITNESSED THE EVENT.

OUR SITUATION WAS GETTING TOO HOT. WE REGROUPED AND THE LIEUTENANT DECIDED TO CALL IRONHAND FOR IMMEDIATE EXTRACTION. IRONHAND OPTED TO CALL IN ARTILLERY ON THE ENEMY TROOPS WE HAD JUST ENCOUNTERED.

ROGER THAT, IRONHAND... GRASSROOTS, CLEAR.

INCOMING ARTILLERY SHELLS CHATTERED OVER OUR HEADS AS THE HUEY SCREWED ITSELF INTO THE EARLY EVENING SKY.

YOU THINK WE RAN FROM A FIGHT? LEFT A BAD TASTE IN YOUR MOUTH? WELL, GET USED TO IT.

THERE IT IS.

NO, I WAS THINKING ABOUT THOSE ARVN PRISONERS.

IT'S LIKE THIS, JOURNAL. THERE'S A POLITICAL ADVANTAGE IN KEEPING AMERICAN POWS ALIVE BUT THERE IS NO SUCH ADVANTAGE IN KEEPING MARVIN ALIVE. WE JUST SPARED THEM WEEKS OF BEING TORTURED TO DEATH IN THE WORST IMAGINABLE WAY. WAR IS NOT PRETTY AND IT'S NOT FAIR... IT'S JUST WAR.

"THERE IT IS". AN ENIGMATIC EXPRESSION OF FRUSTRATION AT THE INANE INSANITY OF WAR.

THERE IT IS.

I HOPED THERE WOULD BE SOME SHOWER WATER LEFT BACK AT THE FIREBASE.

THE END

VIETNAM JOURNAL

by Don Lomax

ONE OF MY SMALL PLEASURES IN VIETNAM WAS WATCHING THE RED DIRT OF THE CENTRAL HIGHLANDS SWIRL DOWN THE DRAIN DURING A LONG SHOWER, A LONG, COLD SHOWER. MY NAME'S SCOTT NEITHAMMER, THE TROOPS CALL ME JOURNAL.

AND, OF COURSE, THE PHONE NEVER RINGS UNLESS YOU ARE IN THE BATHROOM.

THOONT

INCOMIN'!

I SCAMPERED ABOUT, MY NAKED, WHITE ASS IN THE WIND, TRYING TO FIND SOME PLACE TO HIDE FROM THE MORTAR BARRAGE.

OCCUPIED.

GRRR!

I COWERED IN A DITCH TRYING TO CRAWL INTO MY HELMET UNTIL THE ATTACK ENDED AS QUICKLY AS IT BEGAN.

SOON F-4 PHANTOMS WERE NAPALMING THE TREELINE IN AN ATTEMPT TO BRING GRIEF TO AN ENEMY LONG GONE. IT WAS A LONG WALK BACK TO MY BILLET.

HEY JOURNAL ... SMILE.

The End

VIETNAM JOURNAL

by Don Lomax

DECEMBER 1969 WITH THE 11TH ARMORED CAVALRY IN III CORPS. HALF A DOZEN M113 APCs CLATTERED ALONG HIGHWAY 4 TOWARD VANG TAU. WE WERE BAIT.

WHISKEY-TWO-ZERO, NEGATIVE CONTACT.

THE HAIRS BRISTLED ON THE BACK OF MY NECK. IT HAD ALWAYS BEEN MY EXPERIENCE THAT CHARLIE WAS HAPPY TO OBLIGE WHEN THE DARKHORSE WAS LOOKING FOR TROUBLE.

YOU'D BETTER STAY IN THE HOLE, JOURNAL. WE'VE BEEN CATCHIN' SOME HARASSING FIRE OFF AND ON ALONG HERE.

IT'S LIKE A SAUNA IN THIS THING, I CAN'T BREATH...

BUT AS THE LEAD APC TOOK A B-40 ROCKET IN THE STARBOARD LEAD ROAD WHEEL AND GROUND TO A HALT...

DOUBLE DEUCE, WE'RE TAKING FIRE!

...MY KNEES BUCKLED AND I SUCKED WIND, MID-WHINE. THE WHOLE COLUMN ERUPTED IN ROCKET AND SMALL ARMS FIRE.

THE REAR APC WAS LIKEWISE DISABLED TRAPPING THE MIDDLE VEHICLES LIKE DUCKS IN A SHOOTING GALLERY. BUT THIS WAS THE BLACKHORSE REGIMENT AND THEY WERE ASS DEEP IN EXPERIENCE.

THEIR MOTTO? MAKE CONTACT AND *PILE ON!*

CONTINUED...

VIETNAM JOURNAL

by Don Lomax

THE 11TH ARMORED CAVALRY DANGLED THE BAIT, "CHARLIE" BIT, THEN THE TANKS OF THE 2ND BATTALION, BLACKHORSE REGIMENT, LET THE HAMMER FALL.

THOSE ENEMY NOT KILLED WERE DRIVEN BACK FROM THEIR POSITIONS TOWARD THEIR STAGING AREA, A HAMLET A COUPLE OF KLICKS INTO THE SWAMP WHERE THEY WOULD HOPE TO REGROUP.

THEIR PLAN WAS TO HIT THE COLUMN KNOCKING OUT THE POINT AND REAR APCs LEAVING THE TRAPPED MAIN BODY TO THE SYSTEMATIC, MURDEROUS FIRE OF THEIR WELL EXPERIENCED MORTAR TEAMS.

WITH THE UNEXPECTED COMPLICATION OF THE HARD HITTING M-48s CONCENTRATED FIRE THE ENEMY'S MORTAR TEAMS RAIN OF H.E. ROUNDS FELL ON A DESERTED HIGHWAY 4.

BUT IT WAS A DRY HUMP FOR CHARLIE AS OUR APCs DAISY CHAINED AROUND IN A FLANKING MANEUVER...

...A NEARLY IMPOSSIBLE HAT TRICK EVEN CHARLIE WOULD SOON GRUDGINGLY BE FORCED TO ADMIRE IN THEIR FEW REMAINING MOMENTS OF LIFE.

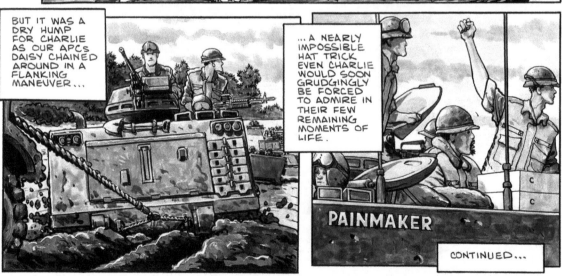

PAINMAKER

CONTINUED...

VIETNAM JOURNAL

by Don Lomax

THE VIET CONG WERE FAMOUS FOR NEVER INITIATING AN AMBUSH WITHOUT SEVERAL POTENTIAL EXITS FROM THE THEATER CONFLICT. A FRUSTRATING ANTICLIMAX FOR THE DARK HORSE REGIMENT... BUT THIS DAY "CHARLIE" FUCKED UP. AN END RUN BY 2ND BATTALION APCs BLOCKED HIS RETREAT...

...WHILE THE 11TH CAVALRY'S M-48S HAMMERED THE TRAPPED ENEMY COMBATANTS.

WHEN RETURN FIRE TRICKLED TO A MINIMUM THE MISSION TO ROOT OUT THE REMAINING ENEMY FELL, AS IT ALWAYS DID, TO THE GRUNTS.

EXPERIENCE HAD LEFT THE TROOPS WITH A STERN APPROACH TO HOUSE TO HOUSE FIGHTING.

FIRE IN THE HOLE!

WHITE PHOSPHORUS...

...AND HOT LEAD...

...BROUGHT AN END TO THE DAY'S WORK.

2 AMERICAN CASUALTIES. 26 VIET CONG DEAD. JUST ANOTHER INCIDENT IN AN ENDLESS WAR.

The End

VIETNAM JOURNAL

by Don Lomax

THE TET OFFENSIVE, THE EASTER OFFENSIVE, DAK TO, AND HAMBURGER HILL WERE ALL BLOODY, MEATGRINDER CAMPAIGNS WHICH USED UP 100 TO 500 YOUNG AMERICANS EVERY WEEK OF THE VIETNAM WAR. BUT THE DAY TO DAY SMALL ACTIONS, UNNAMED AND ONLY REMEMBERED BY THOSE WHO SUFFERED AND DIED THERE, LIKEWISE WASTED AMERICAN YOUTH TO FEED THE DEATH MACHINE.

YOU GOTTA DO SOMETHING, LT.!

WE SCRATCHED FOR COVER IN THE STEEPLY TERRACED PADDIES WITH DEATH SQUATTING IN EVERY HEDGEROW.

CORPORAL! YOU WILL STAND DOWN! MY MORNING REPORT WILL NOT ACCOMMODATE ONE MORE CASUALTY! DO I MAKE MYSELF CLEAR?

THE CLOCK WAS TICKING. POINT MAN, CORPORAL MOORE, LAYING LIKE A CRUMPLED PILE OF LAUNDRY, SOAKED THE SUNBAKED GROUND WITH BLOOD AS BLACK AS MOTOR OIL.

THE FIRE MISSION'S IN SIR... BUT THEY SAY IT'LL BE A-WHILE. NO GUNSHIPS AVAILABLE EITHER... WE'RE PINNED DOWN.

IN THE VENACULAR, "WASTED" MEANT JUST THAT..., A WASTE.

LT., HE'S STILL ALIVE! I CAN GET HIM!

NEGATIVE, DOC! THAT IS A DEAD MAN! CHARLIE HAS THAT PADDY ZEROED! YOU MOVE AND I'LL ARTICLE IS YOUR ASS!

THE THREAT OF AN ARTICLE IS HARDLY INTIMIDATED THE MEDIC!

LET'S GO, DOC... I'LL COVER YOU!

BASTARDS!

BUT A BURST OF AK FIRE CUT THEM DOWN BEFORE THEY HAD COVERED HALF THE DISTANCE TO THEIR FALLEN BROTHER.

DIRTY BASTARD!

AND AGAIN THE ENEMY GUNS FELL SILENT AS THE BAIT TWITCHED AT THE END OF CHARLIE'S LINE.
THE LIEUTENANT KNEW HIS COMMAND WAS UNRAVELING.
AND THE SUN BEAT DOWN 120° STRONG.

CONTINUED...

VIETNAM JOURNAL

by Don Lomax

STAY QUIET, DOC... YOU'LL DRAW FIRE.

THE STAKES HAD GONE UP. THREE MEN LIE WOUNDED IN THE SUNBAKED CLEARING. DOC, HIS LEGS SHATTERED, CRAWLED TO THE CLOSEST, DOWNED TROOPER IGNORING HIS OWN INJURIES.

THE PLATOON TURNED TO THEIR LEADER, LIEUTENANT BROPHY, FUMING. SQUATTING THERE, UNDER COVER, WHILE THEIR BROTHERS BLED TO DEATH WAS MORE THAN GALLING, IT WAS CRIMINAL.

THE LIEUTENANT KNEW HE HAD NO CHOICE BUT TO ACT AND ACT QUICKLY.

ALRIGHT, WHEN I GIVE THE WORD I WANT EVERY WEAPON FIRING ON THAT TREELINE! SURPRESSIVE FIRE OUT THE ASS!

ROSCO, HEAT UP THUMPER! I WANT CHARLIE DOWN IN HIS HIDIE-HOLES FOR A GOOD TWO MIKES!

COMPREHENDO, LT.

JOURNAL...SINCE YOU DON'T HAVE A WEAPON YOU CAN HELP CARRY... CARLOS, O'NEAL, ON MY SIX!

IT WAS THE LONGEST 15 METERS OF MY LIFE. ON THE LIEUTENANT'S COMMAND A FLURRY OF GUNFIRE SHREDDED THE FOLIAGE OPPOSITE OUR POSITION...

AND THUMPER'S HOLLOW REPORT, FOLLOWED BY ITS SIGNATURE THUD, DEVASTATED TEN METER SECTIONS AT A TIME.

COME ON OLD MAN, YOU WANTA LIVE FOREVER?

I WAS HOPING...

CONTINUED...

VIETNAM JOURNAL

by Don Lomax

UNDER THE HAIL OF SUPRESSIVE FIRE WE DARTED OUT AND RETRIEVED THE THREE DOWNED TROOPERS WITH NO FURTHER CASUALTIES.

YOU HAUL ASS FOR AN OLD MAN, JOURNAL.

LIEUTENANT BROPHY HAD DEFUSED THE TINDERBOX SITUATION BUT THAT SUNBAKED PADDY STILL PRESENTED A POSSIBLE KILLING FIELD THREAT TO THEIR ADVANCE.

LT., I GOT "SPOOKY" ON THE HORN. HE NEED CHARLIE'S POSITION AND IS WAITING FOR CLEARANCE TO FIRE FROM "PAWNEE CONTROL".

"SPOOKY". A DEPENDABLE C-47 WEAPONS PLATFORM WITH THREE 7.62 MM MINIGUNS FACING OUT THE PORT SIDE CAPABLE OF FIRING A HAIL STORM OF 6000 ROUNDS PER MINUTE ON AN ENEMY POSITION.

ROGER SPOOKY. IDENTIFY MY SMOKE... CHARLIE'S SQUAT, 150 METERS MY SIERRA WHISKEY.

WATCH THIS, JOURNAL. IT'S A HELL OF A SHOW.

THE MINIGUNS HOWLED AND THE VEGETATION WAS CHOPPED INTO A HORRIFIC SALAD OF DEVASTATION. IN ONLY A MATTER OF SECONDS IT WAS OVER.

LESS THAN AN HOUR LATER THE SITUATION HAD RESOLVED ITSELF ENABLING THE DUSTOFF OF OUR CASUALTIES.

WHEN WE FINALLY WALKED THE BULLET RIDDLED GROUND, ONLY A DOZEN OR SO EMPTY SHELL CASINGS EVIDENCED THE ENEMY PRESENCE.

NO BLOOD TRAILS OR DRAG MARKS... SHIT, CHARLIE WAS LONG GONE BEFORE SPOOKY EVEN SHOWED UP.

SAME OLD STORY. REGROUP, PEOPLE! WE'RE HEADING HOME.

the End

VIETNAM JOURNAL

by Don Lomax

"NIXON EDGED HUMPHREY OUT IN THE NOVEMBER 1968 ELECTION CLAIMING HE HAD A SUREFIRE PLAN TO BRING THE WAR TO AN END AND INITIATE A 'PEACE WITH HONOR' IN VIETNAM."

"IN THE FIRST FEW MONTHS OF 1969 THE BODY COUNT FOR AMERICAN TROOPS WAS AVERAGING 400 A WEEK. ONE WEEK IN MARCH 453 YOUNG AMERICAN SOLDIERS LOST THEIR LIVES."

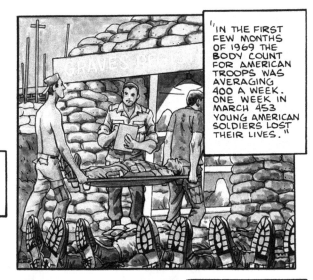

"MACV HAD BEEN BEGGING THE JOHNSON ADMIN-ISTRATION FOR PERMISSION TO CROSS THE CAMBODIAN BORDER AND TAKE THE FIGHT TO THE ENEMY SANCTUARIES AND BASECAMPS FROM WHICH THE NVA FELT SECURE TO LAUNCH THEIR WELL PLANNED OUT ATTACKS AGAINST OUR FORCES."

"NIXON HAD BARELY TAKEN OFFICE WHEN HE AUTHORIZED 'OPERATION MENU' THE CODE NAME FOR AN INTENSE B-52 BOMBING CAMPAIGN TO DESTROY THE THOUSANDS OF TONS OF SOVIET MADE ARMS AND SUPPLIES THE NVA HAD CACHED ON THE CAMBODIAN SIDE OF THE 400 MILE BORDER SEPERATING CAMBODIA AND VIETNAM."

"AT 05:00 WE DEBARK FOR THE FISHHOOK REGION, JUST ACROSS THE BORDER FROM TAY NINH PROVINCE TO ASSESS THE SUCCESS OF OPERATION MENU IN THAT AREA. BUT TONIGHT WE SLEEP THE SLEEP OF THE DEAD NOT KNOWING WHEN WE WILL HAVE OUR NEXT OPPORTUNITY FOR REST.

SCOTT NEITHAMMER, CORRESPONDENT."

WILL YOU PUT THAT NOISY FUCKING TYPEWRITER AWAY AND TURN OFF THE LIGHT?

GOOD-NIGHT, CORPORAL

CONTINUED ...

VIETNAM JOURNAL

by Don Lomax

I COULD TELL THE BRASS WERE EXTREMELY UNCOMFORTABLE HAVING ME AROUND. A LOT OF WHISPERING BEHIND MY BACK IN THE HALLS AT MACV HAD SPARKED MY INTEREST. AFTER AN EXTENDED TIME OF HUMMING AND HAWING I GOT PERMISSION TO TAG ALONG WITH A DAMAGE ASSESSMENT TEAM NEAR THE END OF MARCH 1969.

ROLLING THUNDER CAMPAIGNS ACROSS THE POROUS BORDER INTO LAOS HAD BEEN DOCUMENTED THE YEAR PRIOR BY MYSELF AND OTHER JOURNALISTS. THOUGH RUMORS OF A MAJOR BOMBING INCURSION INTO CAMBODIA WERE FLOATING ABOUT THE EVIDENCE HAD ELUDED ME.

WAIT A MINUTE! YOU'RE NOT THE DAMAGE ASSESSMENT TEAM!

WHO--

THE BORDER IS NOT AS WELL DEFINED ON THE GROUND AS ON A MAP. THE SCENES OF DEVASTATION I WITNESSED COULD HAVE, A COUPLE OF DEGREES ONE DIRECTION, BEEN VIETNAM, BUT A COUPLE OF DEGREES THE OTHER DIRECTION WOULD HAVE PLACED THEM IN CAMBODIA AND RIPE FOR WORLD CONDEMNATION.

YOU'RE NOT EVEN MILITARY, ARE YOU? WHO THE HELL ARE YOU?

THE MORE THEY TRIED TO ASSURE ME EVERYTHING WAS ON THE UP AND UP THE MORE I HAD BECOME A THORN IN THEIR SIDE. AS THE UNMARKED CHOPPER LANDED IN A CLEARING I WAS ASK TO STAND DOWN. THE HAIR ON THE BACK OF MY NECK BRISTLED.

MY PROTESTS FELL ON DEAF EARS. I HAD BEEN SET UP AND THEY WERE MAKING THE PROBLEM (ME) GO AWAY.

THE UNMARKED HUEY SCREWED ITSELF INTO THE SKY. I EXPECTED TO TAKE A FULL BURST FROM THE M-60 ON THE DOOR WITH THEIR DEPARTURE.

BUT AS THE SOUND OF THE CHOPPER FADED IN THE DISTANCE THE FUTURE I WAS FACING SEEMED EQUALLY FINAL.

CONTINUED ...

VIETNAM JOURNAL

by Don Lomax

PRESIDENT RICHARD M. NIXON ORDERED OPERATION MENU, THE BOMBING OF NORTH VIETNAMESE SANCTUARIES IN CAMBODIA, ON MARCH 15, 1969, A MAJOR BOMBING CAMPAIGN AGAINST A SOVEREIGN THIRD COUNTRY.

WHEN I GOT WIND THAT SOMETHING STUNK AT MACV, A COVERT OPERATION OF UNIDENTIFIED, SHADOWY INDIVIDUALS TOOK ME DEEP INTO THE PARROT'S BEAK AND LEFT ME FOR DEAD. THEY OBVIOUSLY EXPECTED ME TO FOLD UP LIKE A CHEAP TENT AND CEASE TO BE A PROBLEM.

I HAD HAD MY ASS IN THE GRASS FOR THE PAST YEAR AND A HALF. DAK TO, TET, THE A SHAU VALLEY HAD TAUGHT ME WELL. I WOULD SURVIVE AND THE SPOOKS WHO HAD DETERMINED THE BEST WAY TO DEAL WITH THE TRUTH WAS TO HIDE IT FROM THE WORLD WOULD BE EXPOSED. THERE IS NOTHING A COCKROACH HATES MORE THAN THE LIGHT.

SUDDENLY I WAS STARING ACROSS THE CLEARING AT A HOLLOW-EYED, LEATHER-SKINNED EUROPEAN. A GAUNT DEATH MASK WITH BURNING EYES THAT CHILLED ME EVEN IN THAT HOT, SMOTHERING UNDERGROWTH.

FROM BEHIND, A RIFLE BUTT STUNNED ME, DROPPING ME TO MY KNEES. I HAVE NO DOUBT THAT THIS BAND OF KHMER ROUGE REBELS WOULD HAVE KILLED ME HAD HE NOT ORDERED THEM TO STOP.

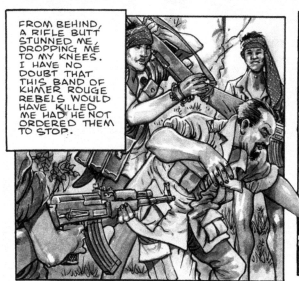

AS I FADED INTO UNCONSCIOUSNESS HE BARKED ORDERS, IN FRENCH, TO THE SQUAD OF KHMER IRREGULARS. ANOTHER MYSTERY IN AN INSANE WAR. NOTHING SURPRISED ME ANYMORE.

CONTINUED ...

VIETNAM JOURNAL

by Don Lomax

IN 1969, NORTH VIETNAMESE TRAINED KHMER ROUGE WERE ON THE THRESHOLD OF A PUSH FOR THE OVERTHROW OF THE SIHANOUK GOVERNMENT IN CAMBODIA LED BY THE INFAMOUS, POL POT.

MY HEAD WAS SPLITTING AS I WAS PRODDED AND HALF DRUG DOWN GREEN, PADDED TRAILS. ILL-TEMPERED AND SINGLE-MINDED, THE KHMER REBELS HAD LITTLE SYMPATHY FOR MY LUMBERING, BREATHLESS ATTEMPTS AT KEEPING UP THE PACE.

THEIR BASE CAMP WAS WELL ESTAB-LISHED WITH WELL WORN TRAILS COMING IN FROM ALL DIRECTIONS. THE CAMP WAS WELL CAMOUFLAGED AND INVISIBLE FROM ABOVE.

AND THE FRENCHMAN? I WOULD NEVER LEARN HIS STORY.

IT WAS SHORTLY AFTER THE BREAKFAST FIRES HAD BEEN LIT WHEN MY NUMBA-ONE TOR MENTOR CAME TO GET ME, CONFIDENT, AND SO SURE THAT SHE COULD HANDLE THIS FAT, INFERIOR WESTERNER BY HERSELF...

I WAS TENDED BY A PAIR OF SURLY WOMEN WHO DELIGHTED IN POKING AND PROD-DING ME AND DEPRIV-ING ME OF SLEEP.

I SPENT FOUR OF THE LONGEST NIGHTS OF MY LIFE IN THAT WET, CRAMPED CAGE UNABLE TO LIE DOWN. I DOZED WHEN I COULD, STANDING.

IT SEEMED I COULD ALWAYS RELY ON EVERYONE UNDER-ESTIMATING ME.

CRACK

MY GENERATION WAS TAUGHT YOU DID NOT HIT A LADY. I RATIONALIZED, THAT LITTLE BITCH WAS HARDLY A LADY.

CONTINUED ...

VIETNAM JOURNAL

by Don Lomax

THUD THUD

I STUMBLED DOWN JUNGLE TRAILS EXPECTING A BULLET SLAM INTO THE BACK OF MY HEAD WITH EACH STEP, WHEN I HEARD THE RATTLE OF SMALL ARMS AND MOTAR FIRE COMING FROM THE KHMER ROUGE BASE CAMP.

A PITCH BATTLE RAGED BETWEEN THE KHMER REBELS AND THEIR ATTACKERS. WERE THERE AMERICANS IN THE PARROT'S BEAK, MISTAKING THE KHMER FOR NVA? NOT LIKELY.
THE ATTACK WOULD HAVE BEEN PRECEDED BY AN INTENSIVE AIR ASSAULT.

ARVN? (ARMY OF THE REPUBLIC OF VIETNAM) NOT A GHOST OF A CHANCE. MARVIN THE ARVN HAD NO BACKBONE FOR SUCH AN ASSAULT.

I KNEW SPECIAL FORCES WERE PROBABLY IN THE AREA BUT THIS, NO HOLDS BARRED, SAVAGE ATTACK WAS NOT THEIR STYLE.

FROM MY HIDING PLACE I ALMOST FELT SORRY FOR THE KHMER IN THEIR DEATH THROES AS EVERY INDIGNATION WAS HEAPED ON THE VANQUISHED INCLUDING RAPING AND BEHEADING THE CORPSES.

WHAT FORCE OF SAVAGE CLARITY COULD HATE WITH SUCH OVERWHELMING FEROCITY? I KNEW AS THEY DRIFTED OUT OF THE JUNGLE AROUND ME.

MONTAGNARDS.

CONTINUED...

VIETNAM JOURNAL

by Don Lomax

MONTAGNARDS, WHICH MEANS MOUNTAIN PEOPLE, A FRENCH TERM DESCRIBING SEVERAL ABORIGINE TRIBES, WERE LOOKED DOWN ON AND EXPLOITED BY JUST ABOUT EVERY PARTICIPANT IN THE DECADES LONG STRUGGLE IN VIETNAM.

THE FRENCH, THOUGH RESPECTFUL OF THEIR FIGHTING ABILITY, TREATED THEM LIKE CHILDREN. THE NORTH VIETNAMESE BUTCHERED THEM WHEN THEY THOUGHT THEY HAD ALLEGIANCE WITH THE SOUTH.

THE SOUTH MISTRUSTED THEM AND TREATED THEM LIKE SECOND CLASS CITIZENS IN THEIR OWN COUNTRY... A PARALLEL OF OUR OWN GOVERNMENT'S POLICIES TOWARD NATIVE AMERICANS IN THE U.S. A CENTURY BEFORE.

DUNG LAI

PERSONALLY, I HAVE NOTHING BUT RESPECT FOR THE WILY, HARD AS NAILS, PLEASANT DIS-POSITIONED "YARDS". FOR TWO DAYS I WAS PASSED FROM OUTPOST TO OUTPOST UNTIL I WAS AGAIN AT THE MACV OFFICES IN SAIGON.

SIR! SIR! THE COLONEL ISN'T SEEING ANYONE...

HE'LL SEE ME!

NEITHAMMER?! LOOK, I HEARD WHAT HAPPENED TO YOU AND I'VE HAD PEOPLE OUT LOOKING FOR...

YOU LYING BASTARD! WHO THE HELL WERE THOSE PRICKS WHO DUMPED ME IN THE MIDDLE OF THE JUNGLE TO DIE?

CIA? PHOENIX? BLACK OPS?

HOLD ON, SCOTT! THERE'S NO WAY TELLING WHO'S TOES YOU'VE STEPPED ON BUT YOU'VE MADE SOME POWERFUL ENEMIES HERE! I HAVE THE RIGHT TO SHIP YOUR SORRY, CIVILIAN ASS BACK TO THE WORLD! IT'S YOUR WORD AGAINST SOME UNNAMED SHADOW OPERATION THAT DOESN'T EVEN EXIST FOR ALL INTENTS AND PURPOSES.

BUT I DON'T WANT TO DO THAT. HELL, I KINDA LIKE YOU, JOURNAL. NO HARM DONE, ALL IS FORGIVEN. SOMETHING BIG IS COMING UP. PLAY BALL AND YOU'LL GET SOME OF YOUR JUICIEST BY-LINES YET. WHATCHA SAY?

'PLAY ALONG, ALL'S FORGIVEN'... I HAD HEARD THAT SHIT BEFORE. BUT PLAYING ALONG WAS PART OF THE GAME. THE INCIDENT WOULD TURN OUT TO BE JUST ANOTHER CHAPTER FOR MY MEMOIRS.

VIETNAM JOURNAL

by Don Lomax

MAY 1969. THAT SAIGON COWBOY OF A COLONEL HAD PROMISED ME SOMETHING BIG WAS COMING UP. BACK HOME PUBLIC OPINION THAT THE WAR WAS LOST WAS BUBBLING OVER INTO THE STREETS AS USUAL. RETURNING SOLDIERS DARE NOT WEAR THEIR UNIFORMS HOME. IN PARIS, DELEGATES FOUGHT OVER THE SHAPE OF THE TABLE FOR THE PEACE TALKS.

THE SAIGON PRESS CORPS WERE PACKING UP THEIR TYPEWRITERS AND T.V. CAMERAS AND LEAVING THEIR SECURE DIGS AT THE CONTINENTAL HOTEL AND HEADING NORTH. THE 'SOMETHING BIG' WAS HAPPENING.

IT'S ALL BULLSHIT... EVERYBODY KNOWS THE WHEELS ARE COMING OFF THIS WAR.

WE'RE GONNA LOSE THIS WAR. THE FIRST WAR AMERICA'S EVER LOST. HOW DO WE LIVE WITH THAT?

I THINK THE KEY WORD THERE IS LIVE!

HOW YOU GONNA LIVE WITH THAT, TROOP? YOU LOCK AND LOAD, STAND TALL, MARCH INTO HELL, AND PISS IN THE DEVIL'S EYE.

I OPTED TO STAY OFF THE PRESS PLANE AND WENT IN WITH THE 101ST. THE A SHAW VALLEY IN I CORPS WEST OF DA NANG WAS, FOR THE MOST PART, UNDER AMERICAN CONTROL. BUT THE RUGGED AP BIA MOUNTAINS AFFORDED THE NORTH VIETNAMESE A REFUGE THAT WAS A CONSTANT THORN IN THE SIDE OF MACV.

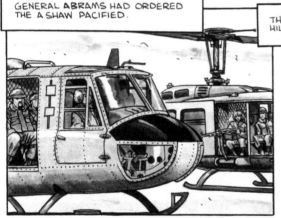

GENERAL ABRAMS HAD ORDERED THE A SHAW PACIFIED.

THEN CAME HILL 973.

"HAMBURGER HILL."

CONTINUED...

VIETNAM JOURNAL

by Don Lomax

CONTACT IN THE A-SHAU VALLEY WAS INCREASINGLY SEVERE THROUGH APRIL AND INTO MAY 1969. 11500 AMERICAN TROOPS LOST THEIR LIVES IN SOUTH VIETNAM IN THAT YEAR AND, "HAMBURGER HILL" IS CONSIDERED THE TURNING POINT IN THE WAR.

IT LOOKED AS THOUGH I WAS GETTING THERE JUST IN TIME FOR THE FEATURE PRESENTATION. THE COMING ATTRACTIONS WERE GRISTLY. I'M NEITHAMMER, THE TROOPS CALL ME 'JOURNAL'.

MACV SANG THE SAME OLD SONG, THE A-SHAU VALLEY WAS KEY AS AN NVA INFILTRATION ROUTE. DEPRIVING THE ENEMY OF ITS ACCESS CRIPPLED THEIR RESUPPLY IN THE SOUTH.

THESE HILLS ARE CRAWLING WITH NORTH VIETNAMESE. YOU BET YOUR ASS WE'RE GONNA BE HERE TILL WE DIG EVERY MOTHER-FUCKING DINK OUTTA THIS VALLEY.

RUMOR SAID WE WAS PULLIN' OUT... RUMOR SAID.

MAY 10. SKIRMISHES AND AMBUSHES INCREASED AGAINST THE SCREAMING EAGLES EVEN AS PREPARATIONS WERE MADE FOR A PUSH UP THE RIDGE LINE TO HILL 937, DONG AP BIA...

THE MEAT GRINDER... SOON TO BE KNOWN AS HAMBURGER HILL.

NO MATTER HOW MUCH THE BATTLEFIELD WAS PREPARED IT WOULD PROVE NOT TO BE ENOUGH.

CONTINUED...

VIETNAM JOURNAL

by Don Lomax

MAY 10, 1969. HAMBURGER HILL. 1800 TROOPS POISED TO TAKE THE FIGHT TO THE NVA DUG IN ON THE SUMMIT OF HILL 937. THE NEXT 10 DAYS WOULD WITNESS SOME OF THE MOST INTENSE ACTION OF THE VIETNAM WAR. BLACKJACK WANTED HIS CP MOVED TO THE TOP OF THE HILL BY THE FOLLOWING DAY.

AIRSTRIKES, ARTILLERY BARRAGES, AND COBRA HELO ASSAULTS POUNDED THE HILL.

WE COULD "FEEL" THE ENEMY PRESENCE EARLY ON AS WE MOVED FROM ONE RIDGE TO THE NEXT. BETWEEN CLUMPS OF TRIPLE CANOPY VEGETATION THE ELEPHANT GRASS SLICED AT US. THE ENEMY WAS IN THE TREES SPOTTING FOR THEIR MORTAR AND RPG TEAMS ...

...THEY WERE POPPING OUT OF SPIDER HOLES BEHIND US...

... AS CLAYMORES IN THE TREES SHREDDED THOSE UNLUCKY ENOUGH TO STUMBLE INTO THEIR CIRCLE OF DEATH.

NIGHT FELL AND WE HUNKERED DOWN... THE ENEMY, A STONE'S THROW BEYOND OUR ESTABLISHED PERIMETER.

THE SMELL OF DEATH AND CHARRED FLESH WAFTED DOWN FROM THE HILL ABOVE.

CONTINUED...

VIETNAM JOURNAL

by Don Lomax

MAY 11, 1969
HAMBURGER HILL

SOLDIERS OF THE 101ST ENDURED AN UNEASY NIGHT'S SLEEP KNOWING THAT WITH THE DAWN THEY WOULD BE EXPECTED TO SLOG TO THE TOP OF HILL 973. WITH "BLACKJACK" HOVERING ABOVE THEM LIKE GOD ALMIGHTY, 1ST PLATOON BEGAN A RECONNAISSANCE IN FORCE ALONG THE RIDGE LEADING TO THE SUMMIT.

DEAD NVA, BLOOD TRAILS, AND DISCARDED, BLOODY BANDAGES INDICATED THE HAMMERING THE ENEMY HAD TAKEN THE DAY BEFORE.

PERIODIC RAINSTORMS DRENCHED THE SLOW MOVING ADVANCE. BLACKJACK COMPLAINED AT THE SLOW PACE. HE WANTED TO BE SITTING ATOP THE HILL BEFORE THE END OF THE DAY.

THROUGH CAPTURED COMMUNICATIONS AND NVA DOCUMENTS THE AMERICANS FOUND OUT EXACTLY WHAT THEY WERE UP AGAINST, THE 29TH NVA REGIMENT. HARD, SHARP, AND READY FOR A SUSTAINED FIGHT.

BACK ON THE HILL, ENEMY CONTACT GRADUATED FROM SNIPER FIRE TO A HAIL OF GUNFIRE ROCKING THE ADVANCING TROOPS BACK ON THEIR HEALS.

RPGS, CLAYMORES, AND MACHINE-GUN FIRE WAS QUICKLY RETURNED WITH EQUAL INTENSITY. THE M-60 GUNNER TOOK A FULL BURST OF AK FIRE IN HIS CHEST. IT ONLY PISSED HIM OFF.

THROWING DOWN HIS DAMAGED WEAPON HE PICKED UP A FALLEN BUDDY'S M-16 AND EMPTIED IT INTO THE SNIPER BEFORE MAKING HIS WAY TO THE REAR.

IT WAS LIKE THAT. MOMENTS OF ASTONISHING HEROISM.

CONTINUED...

VIETNAM JOURNAL

by Don Lomax

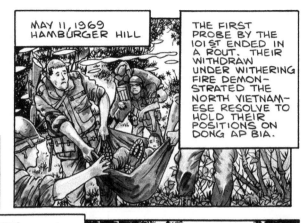

MAY 11, 1969
HAMBURGER HILL

THE FIRST PROBE BY THE 101ST ENDED IN A ROUT. THEIR WITHDRAW UNDER WITHERING FIRE DEMONSTRATED THE NORTH VIETNAMESE RESOLVE TO HOLD THEIR POSITIONS ON DONG AP BIA.

AT THE COMMAND POST THE WOUNDED WERE TREATED AND THE DEAD COVERED WITH PONCHOS WAITING FOR EVACUATION, WHILE ARTILLERY AGAIN POUNDED THE ENEMY POSITIONS FURTHER UP THE HILL.

SUDDENLY, THERE WAS A DRAMATIC INCREASE IN THE PUCKER-FACTOR. TWO COBRA GUNSHIPS MISTAKENLY TARGETED THE CP AND UNLOADED ON THE SIGHT WITH ROCKETS. ONLY THE FIRST FRIENDLY FIRE INCIDENT TO OCCUR ON HAMBURGER HILL.

WITH TWO KILLED OUTRIGHT AND 35 WOUNDED, INCLUDING KEY NCOs, BRAVO COMPANY WAS DECIMATED.

A CALL TO BRIGADE WARNED, WITH A TORRENT OF EXPLETIVES, THAT IF THOSE GUNSHIPS DID NOT DIDI THE AO ASAP THEY WOULD BE SHOT DOWN BY WHAT WAS LEFT OF THE AMERICANS.

AND THERE WAS LITTLE REST THAT EVENING AS ENEMY MORTARS POUNDED THE AMERICAN POSITION, SHREDDING THE BESIEGED TROOPS, UNTIL "SPOOKY" UNLOADED ON THE BAD GUYS WITH A VENGEANCE.

CONTINUED...

VIETNAM JOURNAL

by Don Lomax

MAY 12, 1969
HAMBURGER HILL

THE SECOND ASSAULT ON THE HILL BEGAN BY TAKING DOZENS OF WOUNDED AND DEAD. THIS WAS NO INSIGNIFICANT FORCE THE SCREAMING EAGLES WERE FACING. AS THE DISTANCE UP THE SADDLE-BACK BECAME GREATER BETWEEN RESUPPLY AND THE AMERICAN TROOPS.

AN LZ CLOSER TO THE ACTION WOULD HAVE TO BE ESTABLISHED FOR EVACUATION OF CASUALTIES. ENGINEERS WERE FLOWN IN TO HACK A LANDING ZONE OUT OF THE JUNGLE.

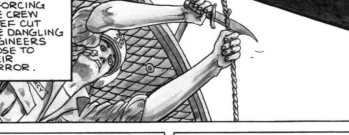

BUT THE CHOPPER TOOK A HAIL OF FIRE FROM THE HONEYCOMB OF ENEMY BUNKERS...

...FORCING THE CREW CHIEF CUT THE DANGLING ENGINEERS LOOSE TO THEIR HORROR.

SATURATION BOMBING PEPPERED THE SITE BEFORE A SECOND ATTEMPT...

WHICH AGAIN ENDED IN DISASTER AS A SINGLE RPG KNOCKED OUT THE MAIN ROTOR AND THE HUEY CRASHED TO EARTH AND CAUGHT FIRE.

THE SURVIVORS SCRAMBLED FOR COVER AS THE HEAVILY LADEN CHOPPER'S AMMUNITION COOKED OFF.

THE SECOND DAY ENDED AS THE FIRST.

CONTINUED...

VIETNAM JOURNAL

by Don Lomax

MAY 13, 1969
HAMBURGER HILL

RUMORS OF A MASSACRE AT FIRE-BASE AIRBORNE WITH 2/501 HAVING BEEN OVERRUN BY HARD-CASE NVA ATTACKERS SPREAD THROUGH THE 350 MEN PRE-PARING TO FACE THE ENEMY FORCE ON DONG AP BIA... HAMBURGER HILL.

THE ENEMY TOOK ON A MYSTIC QUALITY THAT SPOOKED EVEN THE FIERCEST SKY SOLDIER TO SOME EXTENT. CHARLIE DEFINITELY HAD HIS SHIT TOGETHER.

FORWARD AIR CON-TROL REPORTED COOK FIRES ALL OVER THE MOUNTAIN ...HUNDREDS ...CHARLIE WAS COOKING UP A SHITLOAD OF RICE FOR A PROLONGED FIGHT.

THEY'RE THROWIN' SHEEP TO THE WOLVES, SON.

BAAA!

AGAIN THEY PREPARED THE BATTLEFIELD WITH 1000 POUND BOMBS.

AND THOUGH A VALIANT ASSAULT WAS WAGED AGAINST THE ENEMY, THE SCREAMING EAGLES WERE AGAIN FORCED BACK DOWN THE MOUNTAIN DRAGGING THEIR WOUNDED.

LIKE THE DAY BEFORE EVAC CHOPPERS WERE BEATEN BACK OR SHOT DOWN WITH WITHERING FIRE...

RESULTING IN SIX KILLED, SIX SERIOUSLY WOUNDED WITH BROKEN BONES AND THIRD DEGREE BURNS...THE SURVIVORS HAD TO CRAWL OUT CARRYING THEIR WOUNDED OFF THAT MOUNTAIN OF HELL THROUGH A DRENCHING, MISERABLE RAIN.

THE WORLD WAS TAKING NOTICE... THANKS TO A WAR WEARY PRESS OF WHICH I WAS PART.

CONTINUED...

VIETNAM JOURNAL

by Don Lomax

MAY 14, 1969
HAMBURGER HILL

IN POSITION FOR A MAJOR ASSAULT ON THE MORNING OF THE 14TH, AFTER TWO HOURS OF ARTILLERY AND BOMBING, BRAVO AND CHARLIE COMPANIES 3/187TH MOVED ON THE HILL FIRING AS THEY WENT.

GRENADES AND RPGS RAINED DOWN FROM THE 30% INCLINE... SNIPERS IN THE TREES TORE THE ADVANCE APART.

VOLLEY AFTER VOLLEY BROUGHT SNIPERS TUMBLING FROM THEIR NESTS TO DANGLE ON THEIR TETHERS.

ENEMY DEAD FAR OUTNUMBERED THE SKY SOLDIERS... BUT WITH CONSTANT RESUPPLY AND ENEMY TROOPS FRESH TO THE FIGHT ONLY 35 SURVIVORS FROM CHARLIE COMPANY TRICKLED DOWN OFF THE HILL BY THE END OF FIGHTING THAT DAY.
DELTA COMPANY DID NOT FAIR MUCH BETTER.

THE LORD IS MY SHEPHERD...

THEY STUMBLED DOWN THE HILL LIKE ZOMBIES THROUGH A MONSOON RAIN, COMFORTING ONE ANOTHER AS BEST THEY COULD.

BACK IN THE WORLD: WALTER CRONKITE DECLARED, "THE WAR IS LOST..." SENATOR EDWARD KENNEDY TESTIFIED THE COST IN AMERICAN LIVES "SENSELESS AND IRRESPONSIBLE". AND THE TROOPS ON HAMBURGER HILL WERE NUMB, KNOWING THAT WITH THE DAWN THERE COULD BE NO OTHER EVENTUALITY THAN TO SLOG BACK UP THAT BLOODY HILL.

CONTINUED...

VIETNAM JOURNAL

by Don Lomax

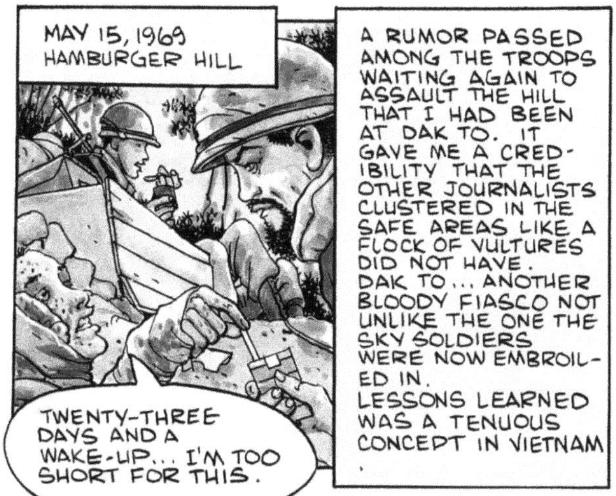

MAY 15, 1969
HAMBURGER HILL
A RUMOR PASSED AMONG THE TROOPS WAITING AGAIN TO ASSAULT THE HILL THAT I HAD BEEN AT DAK TO. IT GAVE ME A CRED-IBILITY THAT THE OTHER JOURNALISTS CLUSTERED IN THE SAFE AREAS LIKE A FLOCK OF VULTURES DID NOT HAVE. DAK TO... ANOTHER BLOODY FIASCO NOT UNLIKE THE ONE THE SKY SOLDIERS WERE NOW EMBROIL-ED IN. LESSONS LEARNED WAS A TENUOUS CONCEPT IN VIETNAM.
TWENTY-THREE DAYS AND A WAKE-UP... I'M TOO SHORT FOR THIS.

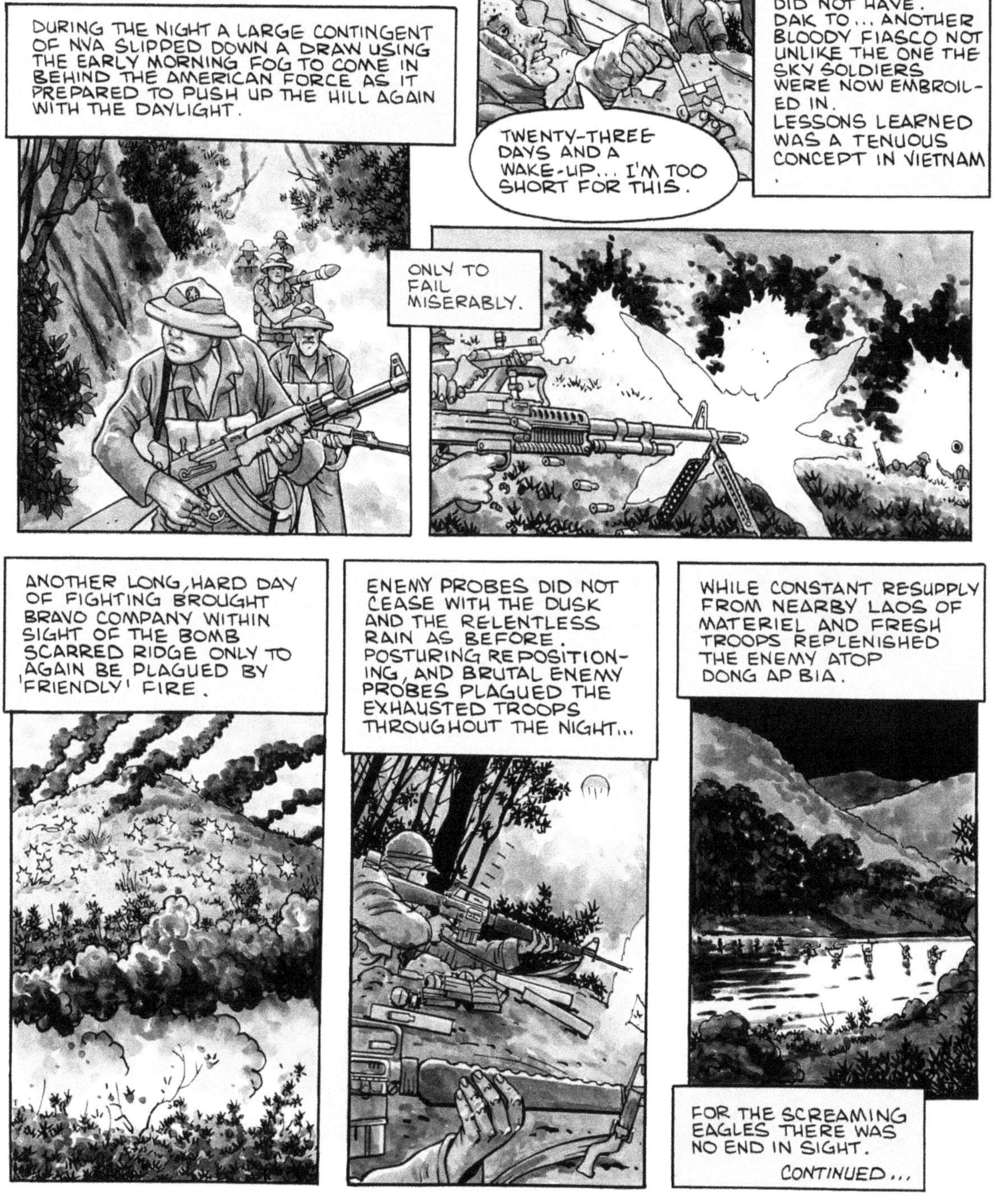

DURING THE NIGHT A LARGE CONTINGENT OF NVA SLIPPED DOWN A DRAW USING THE EARLY MORNING FOG TO COME IN BEHIND THE AMERICAN FORCE AS IT PREPARED TO PUSH UP THE HILL AGAIN WITH THE DAYLIGHT.
ONLY TO FAIL MISERABLY.
ANOTHER LONG, HARD DAY OF FIGHTING BROUGHT BRAVO COMPANY WITHIN SIGHT OF THE BOMB SCARRED RIDGE ONLY TO AGAIN BE PLAGUED BY 'FRIENDLY' FIRE.
ENEMY PROBES DID NOT CEASE WITH THE DUSK AND THE RELENTLESS RAIN AS BEFORE. POSTURING REPOSITION-ING, AND BRUTAL ENEMY PROBES PLAGUED THE EXHAUSTED TROOPS THROUGHOUT THE NIGHT...
WHILE CONSTANT RESUPPLY FROM NEARBY LAOS OF MATERIEL AND FRESH TROOPS REPLENISHED THE ENEMY ATOP DONG AP BIA.
FOR THE SCREAMING EAGLES THERE WAS NO END IN SIGHT.
CONTINUED...

VIETNAM JOURNAL

by Don Lomax

AT FIRST LIGHT AIR STRIKES POUNDED DONG AP BIA AS USUAL. 1/506th MOVED FROM THE VICTORY ON HILL 800 TO JOIN THE BATTLE TAKING SOME OF THE PRESSURE OFF THE 3/187th WHICH HAD TAKEN THE BRUNT OF THE FIGHTING FOR THE PREVIOUS FIVE DAYS.

MAY 16, 1969 HAMBURGER HILL

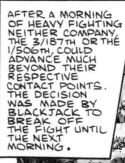

1/506th TOOK HILL 800 TO THE SOUTH OF DONG AP BIA AND EITHER RAN THE ENEMY OFF OR KILLED HIM. THE BATTLE WAS BROKEN BY A BLINDING THUNDERSTORM IN WHICH TWO AMERICANS WERE STRUCK BY LIGHTNING CAUSING ONE TROOPER TO EXCLAIM...

"CHRIST MAN! EVEN GOD'S SHOOTING AT US!"

AFTER A MORNING OF HEAVY FIGHTING NEITHER COMPANY, THE 3/187th OR THE 1/506th, COULD ADVANCE MUCH BEYOND THEIR RESPECTIVE CONTACT POINTS. THE DECISION WAS MADE BY BLACKJACK TO BREAK OFF THE FIGHT UNTIL THE NEXT MORNING.

I WAS AS CONSCIENTIOUS AS POSSIBLE GETTING MY REPORTS OUT, PASSING THEM FROM HAND TO HAND AS BEST I COULD.

I REFUSED TO DELIVER MY NEWS RELEASES IN PERSON TO SAIGON. I WOULD HAVE BEEN TAKING UP SPACE THAT COULD HAVE GONE TO A WOUNDED TROOPER.

I DID NOT KNOW THAT THE WORD WAS ALREADY OUT AND THE PRESS AROUND THE WORLD WERE SECOND GUESSING THE WISDOM OF THE OPERATION AND THE COST IN AMERICAN LIVES.

CAN YOU PASS THIS ALONG FOR ME, SON?

CAN'T GUARANTEE.

UNDERSTOOD.

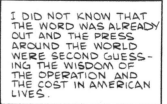

CONTINUED...

VIETNAM JOURNAL

by Don Lomax

MAY 17, 1969
HAMBURGER HILL

WITH MID-MORN-ING CAME THE AIR STRIKES. 1000LB H.E. BOMBS PEPPERED THE ENEMY POSITIONS NOW VISIBLE WITH THE MOONSCAPE SUMMIT, THE RESULT OF DAYS OF SATURATION BOMBING.

HAMBURGER HILL WAS EARNING ITS ANOINTED NICKNAME WITH EACH BEGRUDGED FOOT SOAKED WITH THE BLOOD OF G.I. AND ENEMY ALIKE.

GUNSHIPS SATURATED THE NORTH SLOPE WITH CS GAS FORCING THE ENTRENCHED ENEMY FROM THEIR BUNKERS, CHOKING AND GASPING, ONLY TO BE MET WITH WITHERING FIRE FROM THEIR MINIGUNS.

SKIRMISHES AROUND THE LOWER RIDGES AND RAVINES CONTINUED ERUPTING IN VICIOUS FIREFIGHTS MOST OF THE DAY.

THEN AROUND NOON AN INVASION OF ANOTHER KIND BEGAN. EVERY CHOPPER THAT LANDED CARRIED UP TO A HALF DOZEN NEWS AND MEDIA PEOPLE ON IT. FOR SOME REASON BLACKJACK HAD FOLDED TO PRESSURE FROM THE PRESS.

AND THE INEVITABLE BARRAGE OF STUPID QUESTIONS: "HOW DO YOU FEEL RISKING YOUR LIFE ON THIS HILL WHEN EVERYONE SAYS THE WAR IS ALREADY LOST?"

I HOPE YOU TROOPS DON'T LUMP ME WITH THOSE PUKES.

SHIT, JOURNAL, YOU'RE AWRIGHT ... YOU PAID YOUR DUES WITH YOUR ASS IN THE MUD WITH THE REST OF US.

CONTINUED ...

VIETNAM JOURNAL

by Don Lomax

MAY 18, 1969
HAMBURGER HILL

AIRSTRIKES ON THE MORNING BEGAN LATE THROWING OFF THE SCHEDULED PREP FOR THE REST OF THE MORNING. IT WAS WELL AFTER 10AM WHEN BOTH COMPANIES MOVED OUT TO AGAIN ASSAULT THE HILL. AGAIN INTO THE MEATGRINDER WITH AN OVER-WHELMING SENSE OF DREAD.

THE FIGHTING WAS INTENSE AS THE SKIRMISH LINE SNAKED FORWARD METER BY BLOODY METER.

A STEADY STREAM OF MEDICS BROUGHT DOWN THE WOUNDED THEN RETURNED TO THE FIGHT FOR MORE CASUALTIES.

BY EARLY AFTERNOON THE SCREAMING EAGLES WERE ONLY A FEW HUNDRED METERS FROM TAKING THE HILL. WITH CAUTIOUS OPTIMISM THE BRASS WERE DARING TO HOPE THAT THE END MIGHT BE IN SIGHT.

BUT ONCE AGAIN THE SKY OPENED UP WITH A BLINDING DELUGE THAT BROUGHT THE ADVANCE TO A GRINDING HALT. MUDDY RIVULETS CASCADED DOWN, TURNING THE HILLSIDE INTO A MUDDY WALLOW.

MOVING FORWARD WOULD BE IMPOSSIBLE EVEN IF THE RAIN EASED. HOLDING THEIR POSITIONS FOR THE NIGHT TO CONTINUE THE FIGHT IN THE MORNING WOULD BE SUICIDE. WITH NIGHTFALL AN OVERWHELM-ING COUNTER ATTACK WOULD BE CERTAIN

GRUDGINGLY, THE ORDER TO AGAIN WITHDRAW WAS ISSUED.

MORALE WAS AT AN ALL TIME LOW AND THE USUAL GRUMBLING HAD TAKEN AN OMINOUS TURN WITH A SMATTER-ING OF VOCAL INDIVIDUALS THREATENING TO REFUSE TO GO UP THAT HILL AGAIN.

BUT THEY WOULD GO.
THEY WOULD DO IT ALL AGAIN WITH THE MORNING.

CONTINUED ...

VIETNAM JOURNAL

by Don Lomax

MAY 19, 1969
HAMBURGER HILL

THROUGHOUT THE DAY AND INTO THE NIGHT REPOSITION AND RESUPPLY WERE THE PRIORITY. THE BIG PUSH SCHEDULED FOR THE 20TH WOULD INVOLVE 1/501ST, 2/501ST, 506TH, AND 3/187TH, IN ADDITION TO 2/3 ARVN BATTALION.

BUT BY NO MEANS WAS IT A DAY OFF FOR THE TROOPS. HILL 900 TO THE SOUTH WAS HONEYCOMBED WITH TRENCHLINES AND BUNKERS. MIDMORNING THE 1/506TH PUSHED TO THE TOP.

A SAVAGE FIGHT AS PRIMAL AS ANY TO THAT POINT EVENTUALLY LEFT THE HILL UNDER ALPHA COMPANY'S CONTROL.

SITTING ATOP HILL 900, HAMBURGER HILL SMOLDERED OMINOUSLY 1000 YARDS TO THE NORTH.

BUT BY SUNSET ALL FOUR BATTALIONS WERE POISED FOR THE ALL OUT ASSAULT ON DONG AP BIA THE FOLLOWING DAY.

TOMORROW... I MEAN, YOU THINK THEY'LL BE THERE.

MAYBE THEY'LL JUST DISAPPEAR INTO LAOS TONIGHT ...THEY'VE DONE IT BEFORE.

WE GOT THE TROOPS NOW ...CHARLIE DON'T LIKE A FAIR FIGHT.

DREAM ON.

CONTINUED...

VIETNAM JOURNAL

by Don Lomax

MAY 20, 1969
HAMBURGER HILL

FOR 10 DAYS THE SCREAMING EAGLES CHARGED UP DONG AP BIA. ON THE WESTERN RIM OF THE A SHAU VALLEY JUST A FEW "KLICKS" FROM LAOS, ONLY TO BE BEATEN BACK WITH HIGH CASUALTIES THAT DEMORALIZED THE BATTLE HARDENED PARATROOPERS. FOR SOME IT ONLY TEMPERED THEIR RESOLVE, BUT BATTLE FATIGUE HAD LIKEWISE TAKEN ITS TOLL. A DOOMED FATALISM DESCENDED.

WHAT'RE YOU DOIN', SHANKS?

LEAVE ME ALONE, MAN... I DON'T WANT TO DO IT ANYMORE. WE'RE ALL GONNA DIE ANYWAY!

THINK IT OVER, SHANKS. LET CHARLIE DO IT. SHIT MAN, YOUR MOM AND DAD MIGHT EVEN GET A SHINY MEDAL OUT OF IT TO REMEMBER YOU BY. IF YOU'RE GONNA DIE ANYWAY, GIVE THEM SOMETHING TO BE PROUD OF.

YEAH? JOHN WAYNE THE HELL OUT OF THE MOTHERFUCKER!

I'LL MAKE YOU A PROMISE ...I'LL WRITE ONE HELL OF A STORY TELLING THE WHOLE WORLD HOW YOU DIED LIKE A HERO!

YEAH, BUT JOURNAL... WHAT IF I LIVE THROUGH IT?

IT WAS LIKE THAT. EMOTIONS ALL OVER THE PLACE. FROM THE DARKEST DEPRESSION TO CACKLING LIKE DEMENTED LUNATICS. FROM PERSONAL ACTS OF HEROISM TO RUNNING WITH THEIR TAILS BETWEEN THEIR LEGS.

THEY WERE JUST KIDS, FOR THE MOST PART, WITH THE GRIMMEST OF DUTIES.

SKIRMISHES THROUGH THE NIGHT TESTING OUR PERIMETER WITH B-40 ROCKETS AND GRENADES AFFORDING US LITTLE SLEEP. WITH THE MORNING, THE TROOPS MASSED FOR YET ANOTHER ASSAULT FROM ALL FOUR SIDES.

AND THE BATTLEFIELD WAS AGAIN PREPPED BY TEAMS OF SKYRAIDERS AND F-4S DROPPING HIGH DRAG BOMBS AND NAPALM.

THE MOUNTAIN AGAIN BURNED FROM DOZENS OF FIRES.

AT 10:00 ALL FOUR BATTALIONS MOVED OUT.

CONTINUED...

VIETNAM JOURNAL

by Don Lomax

MAY 20, 1969
HAMBURGER HILL

THE SKIRMISH LINE MOVED FORWARD AFTER EXTENSIVE AIR PREPARATION. FOUR BATTALIONS FROM THREE DIRECTIONS SLOGGED UP THE BLOOD-RED CLAY INCLINE OF DONG AP BIA EXPECTING TO BE CUT TO SHREDS LIKE THE DAY BEFORE. BUT THE SILENCE WAS DEAFENING.

THEY FOUND THE FIRST STRING OF DEFENSIVE BUNKERS DESERTED. SOME TROOPERS WERE EVEN DARING TO HOPE THAT, PERHAPS, THE ENEMY HAD RETREATED INTO LAOS DURING THE PREVIOUS NIGHT.

BUT IT WAS NOT TO BE THAT EASY. THE GODS OF WAR WERE TO DEMAND MORE BLOOD THAT DAY ON THE ALTAR OF HAMBURGER HILL.

AGAIN A HAIL OF RPGs AND GRENADES TOOK THEIR TOLL ON THE ADVANCING TROOPS WHILE BLACKJACK DARTED BACK AND FORTH OVERHEAD DOING HIS THING.

RECOILLESS RIFLE TEAMS MOVED METHODICALLY FROM BUNKER TO BUNKER TAKING THEM OUT. THEY TOPPLED LIKE DOMINOS... THE STENCH OF BURNED FLESH PERMEATED THE HILLSIDE.

JUST LIKE THE NINE DAYS BEFORE, THE WOUNDED CAME DOWN AND REINFORCEMENTS PUSHED UP THE MUDDY TRAILS TO HIT THE LINE, A FRANTIC FRENZY SPREAD THROUGHOUT THE TROOPS... THE SUMMIT WAS IN SIGHT!

NOTHING COULD CHECK THE ADVANCE! 10 DAYS OF HUMILIATION AND FAILURE WAS ENOUGH!

MANY G.I.s WERE ALREADY ON TOP BEFORE THEY EVEN KNEW IT! BLOODIED AND HARD AS TEMPERED STEEL THE SKY SOLDIERS HAD LITTLE COMPASSION FOR THEIR TORMENTORS... THE ENEMY HAD EARNED A QUICK DEATH AND THE AMERICANS COMPLIED!

CONTINUED...

VIETNAM JOURNAL

by Don Lomax

BY THE SUMMER OF 1969 THE WAR I JOINED IN EARLY 1967 LOOKED MUCH THE SAME BUT THE CORE HAD ROTTED FROM A MALIGNANCY OF RACISM, DRUGS, AND THE FEELING THAT ALL WAS LOST WITH NO ONE IN CHARGE.

RACIAL BRAWLS BROKE OUT BETWEEN WHITES, BLACKS, AND HISPANICS WHO HAD SEGREGATED THEMSELVES INTO SEPERATE ARMED CAMPS.

BLACK POWER

THE QUALITY OF OUR MILITARY HAD DECLINED. THE BRIGHTEST AND THE BEST HAD BEEN USED UP. DRAFTEES WHO WERE OFFERED VIETNAM OR JAIL OFTEN CHOSE THE FORMER WHICH FOR MANY WOULD BE A DEATH SENTENCE. NO ONE WANTED TO BE THE LAST AMERICAN KILLED IN THIS STINKING LITTLE WAR.

THEN THE MY LAI MASSACRE CAME TO LIGHT IN MARCH 1969. UNARMED CIVILIANS, OLD MEN, WOMEN, EVEN CHILDREN AND BABIES WERE BUTCHERED BY AMERICAN TROOPS DURING A RAID IN QUANG NGAI PROVINCE BY CHARLIE COMPANY, 1st OF THE 11th INF., AMERICAL DIVISION.

THE NIXON "SECRET WITHDRAWL STRATEGY" THAT HAD GOT HIM ELECTED AND THE VIETNAMIZATION PLANS WERE A COVERUP FOR WHAT WOULD SOON BE A JOKE. THE SOUTH VIETNAMESE DID NOT HAVE THE HEART OR THE WILL TO GO IT ALONE AGAINST HANOI'S MONSTROUS MILITARY MACHINE.

DENT OF THE UN

AMERICANS WERE FIGHTING AND DYING FOR WHAT? WE HAD NEVER LOST A MAJOR CAMPAIGN. THE ENEMY HAD BEEN SOUNDLY BEATEN EVERY TIME HE FACED US AND YET THE PRESS KEPT INSISTING THAT THE WAR WAS LOST.

MORALE WAS AT AN ALL-TIME LOW AS I LANDED AT QUANG TIN 23RD INF. DIVISION HEADQUARTERS (AMERICAL).

REMEMBER, STAY AWAY FROM THE BROTHERS, THEY DON'T MUCH LIKE THE PRESS, THEY'LL FRAG YOUR WHITE ASS.

to be CONTINUED...

VIETNAM JOURNAL

by Don Lomax

MAY 20, 1969
HAMBURGER HILL

BY 1400 HOURS THE MAJORITY OF NVA ON THE HILL TOP WAS EITHER DEAD OR HAD ESCAPED INTO LAOS. IT WAS ESTIMATED BY BLACKJACK THAT LESS THAN A COMPANY REMAINED. THROUGH THE FIGHTING HAD BEEN INTENSE AND COSTLY FOR BOTH SIDES THERE WAS NO DOUBT THE PRIZE WAS THEIRS... HILL 937, HAMBURGER HILL, WAS ABOUT TO BECOME A PART OF HISTORY. ALL THAT REMAINED WAS THAT FINAL PUSH.

FORMING A SKIRMISH LINE THE SKY SOLDIERS MOVED ACROSS THE SUMMIT KILLING ANYTHING THAT MOVED, FRAGGING THE SPIDERHOLES AND BUNKERS IN THE CLEAN-UP. PAYBACK WAS A BITCH.

TOWARD THE CENTER OF THE HILL THEY CAME ACROSS A GROVE OF TORTURED TREES WITH EIGHT NVA STANDING IN A GROUP NOT EVEN ACKNOWLEDGING THE ADVANCING AMERICAN TROOPS. WERE THEY COMMITTING SUICIDE, OR HAD THEY BEEN DRIVEN INSANE BY THE TEN DAY HORROR?

THE TRUTH WAS, NO ONE CARED AT THAT POINT.

WAR IS A HARSH BUSINESS.

600+ ENEMY DIED ON THAT HILL IN THE 10 DAY BATTLE NOT COUNTING ALL THOSE BURIED ALIVE IN COLLAPSED BUNKERS AND SPIDER HOLES AND THOSE WHO LATER DIED OF THEIR WOUNDS IN THEIR LAOTIAN SANCTUARIES.

I DID NOT GO UP TO THE SUMMIT MYSELF. THAT HALLOWED GROUND BELONGED TO THOSE WHO FOUGHT AND DIED UP THERE.

70 AMERICANS DIED AND 372 WERE WOUNDED SPARKING A DEBATE THAT RAGES EVEN TODAY AS TO WHETHER IT WAS ALL WORTH IT.

The End

VIETNAM JOURNAL

by Don Lomax

AFTER A FEW DAYS AT THE AMERICAL DIVISION HEADQUARTERS AT CHU LAI I WAS CRAVING THE BUSH. IT SEEMED THAT EVERYONE WAS EITHER A POTHEAD OR A DRUNK. THE HOOCHES WERE OVERCROWDED AND INFESTED WITH RATS. PASTIMES WERE FIST FIGHTS, BOOZE, POT, AND KILLING RATS.

THE LULL DURING THE SUMMER OF 1969 WAS OFTEN OVERSTATED. G.I.s WERE STILL DYING OUT IN THE BUSH. BUT THE BOREDOM IN THE REAR ECHELONS WAS REAL, PLACATED WITH DRUGS, BOOZE, AND WHORES.

EVERYONE HAD A CHIP ON THEIR SHOULDER AND THE NIGHTS WERE LOUD WITH ROCK MUSIC, DEPRESSION, AND A FATALISM THAT MADE ME WANT TO GET OUT OF THERE ASAP.

I CAUGHT A SHITHOOK TO LZ WEST, ONE OF THE FORWARD CAMPS HOPING TO REPLACE THE INSANITY OF CHU LAI WITH THE INSANITY OF WAR.

AT LEAST THERE WAS SOMETHING BASIC ABOUT WAR. A SIMPLE 'WORK TOGETHER OR DIE' MENTALITY PUT THE PETTY BULLSHIT OF THE REAR ON THE BACK BURNER REPLACING IT WITH A NEED TO SURVIVE.

EXCUSE ME... I'M LOOKING FOR THE XO.

AND THERE WERE STILL SOME WHO HELD TO DUTY, HONOR, AND COUNTRY.

LT. 'WILD BILL' DAVIS... I UNDERSTAND YOU'VE BEEN IN THE SHIT FOR SOMETIME, MR. NEITHAMMER. I'LL DO MY BEST TO GIVE YOU SOMETHING TO WRITE ABOUT.

LT., IT'S A PLEASURE. CALL ME JOURNAL... EVERYONE DOES.

TO BE CONTINUED...

VIETNAM JOURNAL

by Don Lomax

THE FIELD PHONE ERUPTED WITH CHATTER... SOMEONE HAD REPORTED HALF A DOZEN NVA WERE PUTTING TOGETHER A BANGALORE TORPEDO AND ATTEMPTING TO SHOVE IT UNDER THE WIRE.

AUGUST 1969
LZ WEST

THINGS WERE A LITTLE MORE SERIOUS AT THE FORWARD OUTPOST.
A NEIGHBORING FIREBASE, SIBERIA, HAD BEEN MORTARED THE THREE NIGHTS PRIOR AND LZ WEST WAS ON ALERT. I WAS SHARING A DIP WITH THE GRUNTS ON GUARD POST #4 BEFORE TURNING IN.

IT WAS A LITTLE PAST MIDNIGHT. THEN THE SHIT HIT THE FAN.

WHAT? WHERE? NO SHIT...BONER, GET ON THE PIG! THERE'S DINKS AT THE WIRE!

ARTILLERY BEGAN TO CHATTER OVERHEAD FROM THE GUN POSITIONS BEHIND US AND MORE FROM LZ SIBERIA OUR SISTER FIREBASE.

BUT I DETECTED LITTLE OR NO INCOMING FIRE FROM AN ENEMY WE WERE ASSURED WAS OUT THERE. THE TROOPER ON THE 60 BURNED UP BELT AFTER BELT OF AMMO. IT WAS DIFFICULT TO KNOW WHETHER HE WAS FIRING AT SHADOWS OR AN ACTUAL ENEMY. I WAS IN THE WAY, JOSTLED FROM SIDE TO SIDE. HOT BRASS SHOWERED DOWN ON MY EXPOSED FLESH AND DOWN MY SHIRT COLLAR BURNING LIKE HELL.

ARTILLERY FIRE FROM LZ WEST AND SIBERIA POUNDED THE TREELINE. THE ENEMY WAS CAUGHT IN BETWEEN. IT WAS A TURKEY SHOOT. THE ENEMY WAS NO LONGER INTERESTED IN ANYTHING BUT SURVIVAL.

BY DAYLIGHT IT WAS OVER. THERE WAS NOT A SINGLE AMERICAN CASUALTY. INTERROGATED PRISONERS REVEALED THAT THEY WERE UNDER STRICT ORDERS NOT TO ATTACK UNTIL TWILIGHT. WHEN THEIR OFFICERS WERE KILLED IN THE FIRST ARTILLERY BARRAGE THEY HAD NO AUTHORITY TO RETURN FIRE.

THEY WERE MORE AFRAID OF DISOBEYING THEIR OFFICERS THAN THEY WERE OF DYING!

WELL DISCIPLINED LITTLE MOTHER-FUCKERS, WEREN'T THEY?

SPOOKY.

CONTINUED...

VIETNAM JOURNAL

by Don Lomax

SONG CHANG VALLEY. MID-AUGUST. 110 DEGREES. THE TROOPERS OF THE 196TH INFANTRY BRIGADE, AMERICAL DIVISION, WALKED LIKE ZOMBIES UNDER THE WEIGHT OF A FULL LOAD. FOUR DAYS IN THE BUSH AND THEY WERE FINALLY ON THEIR WAY BACK TO LZ WEST WITH ONLY MINIMAL CONTACT WITH THE ENEMY.

THAT WAS TO CHANGE. LATE AFTERNOON THE POINT MAN SPOTTED THREE ENEMY SQUATTING BY A CREEK...FIRE ERUPTED!

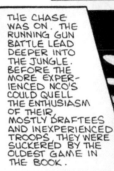

THE CHASE WAS ON. THE RUNNING GUN BATTLE LEAD DEEPER INTO THE JUNGLE. BEFORE THE MORE EXPERIENCED NCO'S COULD QUELL THE ENTHUSIASM OF THEIR, MOSTLY DRAFTEES AND INEXPERIENCED TROOPS, THEY WERE SUCKERED BY THE OLDEST GAME IN THE BOOK.

IT WAS CUSTER'S LAST STAND ALL OVER AGAIN.

LUCKILY, WITH NIGHTFALL THE COMPANY WAS ABLE TO CRAWL AWAY AND REGROUP AT A CRUMBLING FRENCH RUIN THE FOCAL POINT OF A DESERTED HAMLET.

THEY HAD STUMBLED ON TO A SIZABLE FORCE ESTIMATED AT 1200 NVA. DELTA COMPANY'S 100+ TROOPERS WERE SORELY OUTNUMBERED.

to be CONTINUED...

VIETNAM JOURNAL

by Don Lomax

SURROUNDED BY A VASTLY SUPERIOR FORCE, TROOPERS OF THE 196TH INF. AMERICAL DIVISION, BATTLED THROUGH THE NIGHT AGAINST AN ELUSIVE AND EVER ADVANCING ENEMY, TIGHTENING THE NOOSE.

FORWARD OBSERVERS CALLED IN AIRSTRIKES ONLY 50 METERS FROM THEIR OWN POSITIONS.

THE AMERICANS PULLED THEIR PARAMETER EVER INWARD INTO A TIGHT CIRCLE AROUND THE TERRORIZED HAMLET.

THEN I SAW HER STUMBLING, GHOSTLIKE FROM A CAUSTIC CLOUD OF SMOKE.

DO HER, MAN! DO HER! SHE'S A SAPPER!

SHE'S JUST A KID, FOR CHRIST'S SAKE!

SHE'S A FUCKING SAPPER, JOURNAL!

OH, GOD!

I FOUND A MEDIC AS QUICKLY AS I COULD UNDER THE HAIL OF GUNFIRE.

ONLY TO HOLD HER HAND AS SHE SLIPPED AWAY. THE SCARY PART... I COULDN'T EVEN CRY.

SORRY, JOURNAL.

DOC, OVER HERE!

to be CONTINUED...

VIETNAM JOURNAL

by Don Lomax

THE 196TH INF. AMERICAL DIVISION, HAD SUFFERED 10 DEAD AND TWENTY WOUNDED. THE WOUNDED WERE GATHERED TOWARD THE CENTER OF THE LOOSELY FORTIFIED PERIMETER. A DUST-OFF WOULD BE TRICKY UNDER FIRE. WHILE COBRAS ORBITED PROVIDING COVER THE EVAC CHOPPER SWOOPED IN GUIDED BY SMOKE.

AS THE CHOPPER SETTLED INTO THE CLEARING ENEMY FIRE RAKED THE HUEY IN THE EARLY EVENING TWILIGHT SCATTERING THE TROOPS ON THE GROUND.

WITH THE REAR ROTOR DAMAGED THE PILOT TWISTED THE CRIPPLED BIRD BACK INTO THE SKY AND LIMPED OFF TOWARD LZ WEST.

A SECOND ATTEMPT WAS MADE SHORTLY AFTER DUSK. WE ALL HELD OUR BREATH AS THE SECOND DUST-OFF SETTLED TO EARTH A SITTING DUCK FOR ENEMY MORTARS.

AFTER SEVEN WOUNDED WERE ABOARD THE PILOT LIFTED SLIGHTLY, THEN EASED BACK DOWN SHOUTING HE COULD TAKE ONE MORE.

SATISFIED HE COULD CARRY NO MORE, THE PILOT COAXED THE SLICK INTO THE BLACK NIGHT TOWARD THE HOSPITAL AT CHU LAI.

GONNA BE ANOTHER LONG NIGHT.

POSI-GODDAMN-TIVELY.

to be CONTINUED...

VIETNAM JOURNAL

by Don Lomax

REINFORCEMENTS WERE CHOPPERED IN TO RELIEVE THE BESIEGED TROOPS OF THE 196TH.

THEY CALL IT "MILLION DOLLAR HILL" FOR THE NUMBER OF CHOPPERS SHOT DOWN IN ONE DAY DURING THE BATTLE TO TAKE THE VALLEY FROM NATHANIEL VICTOR A WHILE BACK.

BITCHIN'.

THEY OFF-LOADED IN A CLEARING...A FOUR KLICK HUMP IN THE DARK OF NIGHT.

THEY FOLLOWED THE MUFFLED SOUNDS OF BATTLE AND KNEW THEY WERE GETTING CLOSE. THE METALLIC CRUNCH UNDER FOOT OF SHELL CASINGS FROM COBRA GUNSHIPS AND BLOODY DRAG MARKS LEFT BY ENEMY CASUALTIES TESTIFIED TO THE INTENSITY OF THE BATTLE.

AS THE RELIEF TROOPS FILED IN THEY WERE MET LIKE CONQUERING HEROS.

POLES WERE CUT AND THE DEAD WERE PREPARED TO BE CARRIED OUT.

CAN I HELP?

DAMN RIGHT, YOU CAN! WE'RE ALL GOVERNMENT MULES THIS TRIP.

AS WE CONGREGATED TO MOVE OUT THE CHANCES WE WOULD WALK OUT WITH THE SAME LUCK OUR RESCUERS ENJOYED COMING IN THROUGH A BATTALION OF ENEMY TROOPS SEEMED TOO MUCH TO HOPE FOR.

IT WAS.

to be CONTINUED...

VIETNAM JOURNAL

by Don Lomax

IT WOULD BE A FOUR KILO-METER FORCED MARCH, AT NIGHT, FOR THE CUTOFF PLATOON TO LINK UP WITH THE MAIN FORCE. DANCING SHADOWS, STRANGE SHAPES, AND FRAYED NERVES WARNED OF NVA AMBUSHES BEHIND EVERY BUSH OR PADDY BERM.

IN THE DARK IT WAS HARD TO KEEP THE RUBBERNECKING GRUNTS LOADED UP TIGHT, ESPECIALLY CROSSING A WIDE, ANKLE DEEP STREAM. SPORADIC GUNFIRE BROKE OUT SEVERING THE COLUMN AND LEAVING THE STRAGGLERS CUT OFF.

THE AMERICANS TRADED GUNFIRE AND GRENADES FOR THE BETTER PART OF AN HOUR WITH THE INVISIBLE ENEMY. THE WHOLE COLUMN WAS STALLED UNTIL THE REMAINDER OF THE FORCE COULD JOIN THE MAIN BODY.

BUT THE ASSAULT IN FORCE THEY WERE EXPECTING NEVER MATERIAL-IZED AND THE ENEMY, AGAIN, SIMPLY FADED AWAY.

IT WAS A HARD DECISION TO LEAVE THE BODIES BEHIND, BUT THERE WAS LITTLE CHOICE. WE WOULD HAVE TO MOVE FAST NOW WITH OUR PRESENCE KNOWN TO THE NVA.

THE CUTOFF TROOPS SPOOKED AND BOLTED IN THE DIRECTION OF THE REST OF THE COLUMN.

I RAN TOO... MY SKIN CRAWLED AT THE THOUGHT OF BEING LEFT BEHIND. THE TROOPS PANICKED BUT THEN SO DID I AND I WAS TWICE THEIR AGE.

FEAR IS CONTAGIOUS.

to be CONTINUED ...

VIETNAM JOURNAL

by Don Lomax

AS ENEMY MORTARS POUNDED THE RIVER CROSSING BEHIND US, I RAN IN A BLIND PANIC WITH THE REST OF THE CUT OFF SQUAD. DISCIPLINE WAS OUT THE WINDOW. WE COULD HAVE RAN DIRECTLY INTO THE ARMS OF THE NVA, OR HAVE BEEN SHOT BY OUR OWN TROOPS.

WE MUST HAVE SOUNDED LIKE A HERD OF WOUNDED BUFFALO CRASHING THROUGH THE ELEPHANT GRASS. PROBABLY THE ONLY THING THAT SAVED US. THE MAIN BODY KNEW IT WASN'T THE ENEMY. THEY WERE BETTER DISCIPLINED.

GET A HOLD OF YOURSELF TROOP, FER CHRIST'S SAKE!

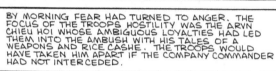

WHAT ABOUT YOU, JOURNAL? YOU'VE BEEN IN THE SHIT BEFORE ...COMBAT VETERAN OF KOREA...

YOU HAD TO BE THERE. SPOOKY NIGHT.

IT WAS AROUND 3 AM WHEN OUR PLATOON LINKED UP WITH THE MAIN COMPANY. IT BROUGHT SOME COMFORT THOUGH WE WERE STILL SURROUNDED BY OVER A BATTALION OF NVA.

FRONT TOWARD ENEMY

BY MORNING FEAR HAD TURNED TO ANGER. THE FOCUS OF THE TROOPS HOSTILITY WAS THE ARVN CHIEU HOI WHOSE AMBIGUOUS LOYALTIES HAD LED THEM INTO THE AMBUSH WITH HIS TALES OF A WEAPONS AND RICE CASHE. THE TROOPS WOULD HAVE TAKEN HIM APART IF THE COMPANY COMMANDER HAD NOT INTERCEDED.

HE WAS SENT OUT ON ONE OF THE CHOPPERS THAT DELIVERED OUR REINFORCEMENTS, CHARLIE COMPANY, 2D BATTALION, 1ST INFANTRY, FOR HIS OWN SAFETY ALONG WITH ALL THE DEAD AND WOUNDED. BUT THE BATTLE WAS HARDLY OVER.

to be CONTINUED ...

VIETNAM JOURNAL

by Don Lomax

PREVIOUS WARS, WWI, WWII, KOREA, WERE WARS OVER TERRAIN, BLOOD SOAKED GROUND WON AND LOST. VIETNAM WAS A WAR OF ATTRITION. BODY COUNT. KEEPING SCORE WITH BODY BAGS. AFTER THE '68 TET OFFENSIVE THE VIET CONG PRETTY MUCH CEASED TO EXIST AS A VIABLE ENEMY. BY MID-SUMMER '69 THE WAR WAS, FOR THE MOST PART WITH NVA REGULARS.

BACK AT LZ WEST I BRAVED THE HUSTLE AND BUSTLE OF REFITTING TO CATCH A QUICK SHOWER AND A HOT MEAL.

I COLLAPSED ON THE NEAREST COT AND PASSED OUT.

15 HOURS LATER I AWOKE TO FIND MY WALLET AND MY BOOTS MISSING. IT WAS GREAT TO BE BACK IN CIVILIZATION.

WHEN I MADE IT BACK TO THE PAD WITH A NEW PAIR OF JUNGLE BOOTS, TWO SIZES TOO SMALL, I FOUND A RIDE WITH A LOAD OF BIG EYED, GREEN TROOPS DESTINED FOR THE A-SHAU VALLEY.

THROUGH IDLE CHATTER I FOUND ONE OF THE TROOPS COMPLAINING THAT HIS BOOTS WERE TWO SIZES TOO BIG. I HAPPILY TRADED WITH HIM. MY LUCK WAS IMPROVING.

To be CONTINUED...

VIETNAM JOURNAL

by Don Lomax

AUGUST 12, 1969. IT WAS MISERABLY HOT AND DRY. THE FIGHTING HAD BEEN INTENSE FOR DAYS WITH AN ILLUSIVE, SIGNIFICANT ENEMY FORCE AS RESILIENT AS SPRING STEEL. I TRADED CHOPPERS AT AN IMPROVISED BATTALION LZ AT THE MOUTH OF AK VALLEY AND CAUGHT A DUST-OFF FERRYING AMMO, FOOD, AND WATER TO THE BESIEGED TROOPS FURTHER UP THE VALLEY.

I THOUGHT ABOUT TAKING A DRINK BECAUSE IT WAS UNBEARABLY HOT BUT THOUGHT BETTER OF IT. TWO CANTEENS OF WATER AND A FANNY PACK FULL OF "C's WOULDN'T LAST LONG IN THAT HEAT.

THE UNARMED HUEY WAS A MAGNET FOR ENEMY FIRE AS WE DROPPED INTO THE CLEARING. FRANTICALLY WE KICKED OUT THE SUPPLIES AND LOADED WOUNDED UNDER FIRE.

THE WATER, FOOD, AND AMMUNITION WERE GONE IMMEDIATELY AS THE CHOPPER QUICKLY ROSE THROUGH THE SMATTERING OF ENEMY FIRE AND WAS GONE.

THEY CAME OUT OF THE BRUSH LIKE GAUNT, EMACIATED GHOSTS. I FROZE. THEY HARDLY LOOKED HUMAN. THE LONG DAYS AND NIGHTS OF FIGHTING HAD LEFT THEM BARELY ALIVE.

WITHOUT A WORD THEY DELIBER-ATELY RELIEVED ME OF MY FOOD AND WATER AS THOUGH I WERE COMPLETELY INCONSEQUENTIAL...

...AND FADED BACK INTO THE BUSH.

I HAD BEEN ROBBED.

I WISHED I HAD TAKEN THAT DRINK EARLIER.

to be CONTINUED...

VIETNAM JOURNAL

by Don Lomax

THE 199th LIGHT INFANTRY BRIGADE ARRIVED IN SOUTH VIETNAM, REPUBLIC OF, DEC. 10, 1966. THOUGH SERVING WITH DISTINCTION UNTIL OCT. 11, 1970. ITS INTENSE, BLOODIED, HOUSE TO HOUSE BRAWL IN SAIGON WITH THE VIET CONG DURING THE 1968 TET OFFENSIVE BROUGHT THE BRIGADE A PROMINENT PAGE IN HISTORY.

AFTER MIDNIGHT JANUARY 31, 1968 A PLATOON SIZE FORCE OF AN ELITE VIET CONG SAPPER BATTALION RETRIEVED THEIR STOCKPILED WEAPONS IN DOWNTOWN SAIGON.

AROUND 3 AM B-40 ROCKETS BLEW HOLES IN THE OUTER WALL OF THE AMERICAN EMBASSY BRINGING THE WAR TO SAIGON.

DURING THE TET TRUCE ATTACKS AGAINST MOST PROVINCIAL CAPITALS AND AMERICAN AND ARVN MILITARY BASES TURNED THE MAJORITY OF THE COUNTRY INTO A BLOODBATH.

THOUGH THE VIET CONG CLAIMED TO FIGHT FOR THE LIBERATION OF THE POPULACE, CIVILIAN MEN, WOMEN, AND CHILDREN WERE BUTCHERED WITH INDIS-CRIMINATE EASE.

THE 199th LIGHT INFANTRY BRIGADE AT LONG BINH FOUND ITSELF FULLY ENGAGED WITH THE 275th VIET CONG REGIMENT.

THE BRIGADE'S 3RD OF THE 7th WAS AIRLIFTED TO PHU THO WHERE THE ENEMY HAD SET UP ITS COMMAND POST AT THE RACE TRACK.

EIGHT HOURS OF INTENSE FIGHTING LIBERATED THE RACETRACK AND THE NEXT TWO DAYS WITNESSED A BLOODY HOUSE TO HOUSE CAMPAIGN AS BRUTAL AS ANY FACING THE MARINES IN HUE.

CHOLON, SAIGON'S CHINATOWN, WAS REDUCED TO CHARRED RUBBLE FROM THE BOMBS AND ROCKETS OF BOTH ARMIES. THE POLITICIANS AND AMERICAN PRESS CALLED TET A DEFEAT, YET EVERY ADVANCE WAS BEATEN BACK AND NOT A SQUARE INCH REMAINED IN ENEMY HANDS.

TROOPERS OF THE 199th WERE AWARDED NUMEROUS COMBAT CITATIONS AND MEDALS INCLUDING FOUR MEDALS OF HONOR. THE BRIGADE LOST 657 SOLDIERS KILLED IN ACTION WITH 2571 WOUNDED IN ITS NEARLY FOUR YEARS INCOUNTRY.

DON LOMAX

A look at the creator of Vietnam Journal

Don Lomax has established himself with Vietnam Journal, his project of two decades which continues today. The series is a rarity in comics in that it appeals not only to comic fans but also to those outside the traditional realm of comics.

But Don is by no means a one trick pony. For nearly 40 years he has had comics and cartoons appearing in a score of national magazines on a regular basis including Easyrider, CARtoons, Heavy Metal, Overdrive, Police and Security News, American Towman, and many others. His work in the adult magazine realm is legendary with story illustrations, comics, and cartoons appearing in virtually every "slick", "girly magazine" imaginable. But he also worked for most of the major comic book imprints including Pacific, Marvel, First, Americomics, Fantagraphics, Eros and others. He said he enjoyed working on American Flagg written by Alan Moore and inking Tom Sutton's pencils on Sleepwalker from Marvel. A multi-talented creator, Don also did some work on Munden's Bar which was a regular feature in First

Lomax based Vietnam Journal on his experiences on his tour of duty in Vietnam in the mid 1960's. He utilizes a war correspondent, to chronicle the combat experiences of the soldiers. Each issue spotlights a soldier or event with the narrative flowing to create story arcs.

The School Library Journal provides an insightful summary of the series. "Sent to Vietnam to report on the conflict, Scott "Journal" Neithammer expects to do no more than produce another sterilized war report. However, he soon realizes that, "the real story was in the bush with the slime, the stink, the constant fear and frustration." Each episode is a mix of the absurd and horrific as Journal befriends an ever-changing cast of doomed soldiers. As he confronts the death, illogic, and contradiction around him, he becomes as conflicted as the war itself, finally losing his journalistic objectivity in a fit of frustrated rage. The black-and-white artwork is powerful, and Journal's world is a rumpled fusion of realism and caricature. "

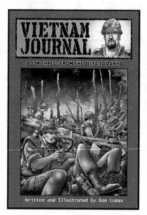

ALSO AVAILABLE FROM CALIBER COMICS

QUALITY GRAPHIC NOVELS TO ENTERTAIN

THE SEARCHERS: VOLUME 1
The Shape of Things to Come

Before League of Extraordinary Gentlemen there was The Searchers. At the dawn of the 20th century the greatest literary adventurers from the likes of Wells, Verne, Doyle, Burroughs, and Haggard were created. All thought to be the work of pure fiction. However, a century later, the real-life descendants of those famous adventurers are recruited by the legendary Professor Challenger in order to save mankind's future. Collected for the first time.

"Searchers is the comic book I have on the wall with a sign reading - 'Love books? Never read a comic? Try this one! ....money back guarantee..." - Dark Star Books.

WAR OF THE WORLDS: INFESTATION

Based on the H.G. Wells classic! The "Martian Invasion" has begun again and now mankind must fight for its very humanity. It happened slowly at first but by the third year, it seemed that the war was almost over... the war was almost lost.

"Writer Randy Zimmerman has a fine grasp of drama, and spins the various strands of the story into a coherent whole... imaginative and very gritty."
- war-of-the-worlds.co.uk

HELSING: LEGACY BORN

From writer Gary Reed (Deadworld) and artists John Lowe (Captain America), Bruce McCorkindale (Godzilla). She was born into a legacy she wanted no part of and pushed into a battle recessed deep in the shadows of the night. Samantha Helsing is torn between two worlds...two allegiances...two families. The legacy of the Van Helsing family and their crusade against the "night creatures" comes to modern day with the most unlikely of all warriors.

"Congratulations on this masterpiece..."
- Paul Dale Roberts, Compuserve Reviews

"All in all, another great package from Caliber."
- Paul Haywood, Comics Forum

HEROES AND HORRORS

Heroes and Horrors anthology provides nine rarely seen or never-before-published heroic and horrifying comic stories from the mind of veteran comic writer Steven Philip Jones.

Featured are entertaining stories with art by Octavio Cariello (The Action Bible), S. Clarke Hawbaker (Nomad), Christopher Jones (Young Justice), Dan Jurgens (Death of Superman), and many more! Foreword by Phil Hester.

"Incredibly creative...Steve's stories are masterworks of what new comics should be: absorbing and exciting and read again and again." - Clive Cussler, international bestselling author.

DAYS OF WRATH

Award winning comic writer & artist Wayne Vansant brings his gripping World War II saga of war in the Pacific to Guadalcanal and the Battle of Bloody Ridge. This is the powerful story of the long, vicious battle for Guadalcanal that occurred in 1942-43. When the U.S. Navy orders its outnumbered and outgunned ships to run from the Japanese fleet, they abandon American troops on a bloody, battered island in the South Pacific.

"Heavy on authenticity, compellingly written and beautifully drawn."
- Comics Buyers Guide

BECK and CAUL INVESTIGATIONS:
Where the Nightmares Walk

- Collects the entire Beck & Caul series for the FIRST TIME!

There is a place where evil lives. Where all of mankind's nightmares are a reality. It is the Underside. From this realm of myth and shadow was born Jonas Beck who teams up with a young woman, Mercedes Guillane and their paths meld into one...to battle evil in all its guises. Set in the voodoo influenced city of New Orleans, Beck and Caul are paranormal detectives who scrounge the streets of this dark, mystical city in order to combat and protect people from supernatural attacks and events.

COUNTER-PARTS

From best selling author Stefan Petrucha (MARVEL's Deadpool, Captain America). Think people can be disingenuous? Of course and in the future they try on new personas like hats. But when Hieronymus Jones overdoses on TPGs (temporary personality grafts), his original personality is destroyed. Now an experimental cure gives him not 1, but 6 new personalities. Each inhabiting a different part of his body. There's: Bogey, the hard-boiled right arm; Kik-li, the Kung-Fu master right leg; Jake, the self-involved torso; Buckley, the too-smart head; Don, the romantic left arm and; Tootsie, the femme fatale left leg! Together, they fight corruption & crime as one strange superhero team. Strap yourself in for one wild ride!

VELDA: GIRL DETECTIVE - VOL. 2

A unique take on the more lurid of the 1950s crime comics as if it actually existed as a Golden Age comic. More than a homage to noir films and hard-boiled detective writing of the 50s it includes in issues features such as a Velda paper doll kit & complete '52 Velda pinup calendar. Also added are vintage ads to amuse readers and shorts such as "Hawkshaw Hawk, Bird Detective" and "Neolithica: Girl of the Pleistocene" ."Velda is the kind of detective I like."- Richard S. Prather (writer, Shell Scott novels). "A pulp classic! If you like your action gritty, yet full of surprises, then you'll love Velda..." - Rick Overton (writer, Dennis Miller Show). "The Velda Comic is spectacular.." - Bob Burns.

CALIBER
COMICS

www.calibercomics.com

CPSIA information can be obtained
at www.ICGtesting.com
Printed in the USA
LVHW111515110122
708310LV00008B/745